D1512297

FIVEST★R SERVICE

SERVICE

your guide to
hospitality excellence

by evan goldstein, MS

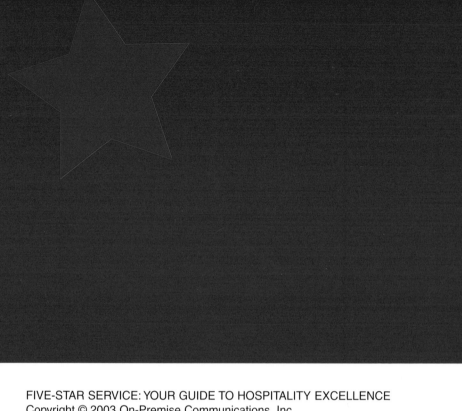

FIVE-STAR SERVICE: YOUR GUIDE TO HOSPITALITY EXCELLENCE
Copyright © 2003 On-Premise Communications, Inc.

ISBN 0-615-12506-9
Printed in China
For information or to purchase additional copies of this book contact:

On-Premise Communications Inc.
100 South Street
Bennington, VT 05201
(802)442-6771
www.info@santemagazine.com

★ CONTENTS

Foreword *1*

Introduction *3*

1 Customer Service

Are you ready for today's customers? *8*

Who is today's diner? *10*

What do Danny Meyer, Joyce Goldstein, and Wolfgang Puck
   have in common? *12*

Details, details, details. *14*

Mastering table service will set you apart from the
   competition. *16*

It's showtime! *18*

It's showtime, act two! *20*

Those all-important first and last impressions. *22*

Complaints should always be met with gratitude. *24*

Word-of-mouth referrals are important. *26*

Few occupations are as stressful as being a server. *28*

Customers we love to hate. *30*

2 Marketing

What makes you so special? *34*

You can't do too much for your best customers. *36*

What sets the best restaurants apart? *38*

How many ways can you say, "May I help you?" *40*

Trends mean change—for the better! *42*

What's the most valuable piece of restaurant
   equipment you own? *44*

At tax time, practice "compassionate opportunism." *46*

3 Human Resources

What is the number one issue facing restaurateurs? *50*

Do you have a winning team? *52*

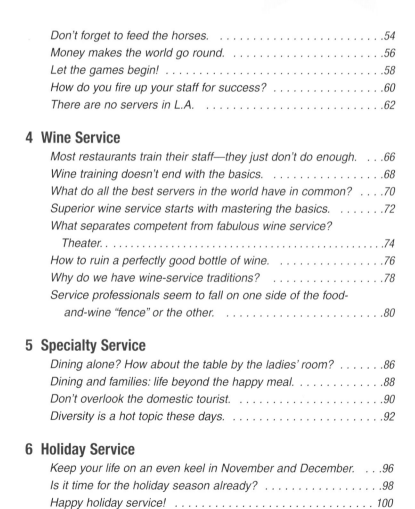

Don't forget to feed the horses. 54

Money makes the world go round. 56

Let the games begin! 58

How do you fire up your staff for success? 60

There are no servers in L.A. 62

4 Wine Service

Most restaurants train their staff—they just don't do enough. . . .66

Wine training doesn't end with the basics. 68

What do all the best servers in the world have in common? 70

Superior wine service starts with mastering the basics. 72

What separates competent from fabulous wine service?
    Theater. 74

How to ruin a perfectly good bottle of wine. 76

Why do we have wine-service traditions? 78

Service professionals seem to fall on one side of the food-
    and-wine "fence" or the other. 80

5 Specialty Service

Dining alone? How about the table by the ladies' room? 86

Dining and families: life beyond the happy meal. 88

Don't overlook the domestic tourist. 90

Diversity is a hot topic these days. 92

6 Holiday Service

Keep your life on an even keel in November and December. . . .96

Is it time for the holiday season already? 98

Happy holiday service! 100

As study after study has shown, the level of service a restaurant provides leaves the most lasting impression on its customers.

 **FOREWORD**

It is my great pleasure to introduce *Five-Star Service: Your Guide to Hospitality Excellence*, written by Master Sommelier and hospitality guru Evan Goldstein. This book addresses one of the most crucial aspects of the restaurant and hospitality business: SERVICE.

As study after study has shown, the level of service a restaurant provides leaves the most lasting impression on its customers. From how the staff members answer the phones and take reservations to the way they bid farewell, and everything in between, guests remember how they are treated long after they forget an establishment's food, beverages, and decor. As is made clear in this book, service details such as these speak volumes about how an enterprise is managed and its approach to customer service.

I can think of no one in the industry better suited to write this book than Evan Goldstein. The son of San Francisco–based Chef Joyce Goldstein, Evan literally grew up in restaurants. As a young man, he apprenticed as a chef in Paris, where, as part of his training, he was required to work the front of the house as a server. After working in Europe for two years, he returned to California to launch Auberge du Soleil with the famed Masa Kobayashi, and subsequently landed at Chez Panisse with living legend Alice Waters. After a few years at Chez Panisse, Evan joined forces with Joyce to open Square One, which quickly became one of the hottest dining spots in the San Francisco area. As the restaurant's general manager, Evan was responsible for all aspects of customer service. From Square One, he went on to found the Sterling Vineyards School of Service and Hospitality, which in its seven-plus years of operation graduated more than 15,000 alumni. More recently, Evan created the Allied Domecq Wines USA Academy of Wine & Service Excellence, an institution dedicated to educating restaurant employees in the fundamentals of wine, wine service, and dining room service.

The chapters in this book are drawn from Evan's "Five-Star Service" column, which has appeared in every issue of *Santé* since its inception. Together they comprise an excellent primer on service for the restaurant management novice and an invaluable reference tool and training resource for the seasoned professional. As I am sure you'll agree, within these pages is a wealth of ideas and information, all of which can help you create a memorable dining experience for your customers and will also help you take more money to the bank.

Mark Vaughan
Editor and Publisher
Santé, the Magazine for Restaurant Professionals

★ INTRODUCTION

Bad service happens all by itself; good service has to be managed.

The customer flagged down her waiter to emphasize how poor the service had been. The waiter turned, smiled, and replied, "How do you know? You haven't gotten any yet." Sigh. This is not a true story, but all service-staff employees and diners can relate to such a predicament.

Poor service is not a novelty in contemporary America, and customers have become increasingly less tolerant of it. And while it's easy to make excuses, find fault in others, or even blame the customers themselves, we all are keenly aware that when it comes to our guest interactions in the dining room, an ounce of prevention is worth far more than a pound of cure.

This notion seems so obvious to most of us. But it has become vividly clear to me over the past dozen-plus years that when it comes to service, many hospitality people simply lack a keen sense of the obvious. Perhaps that's why my columns and what became this guide all started.

A Partnership Evolves

In the fall of 1995, Mark Vaughan, publisher-to-be of *Santé*, and I were having a cup of coffee in downtown St. Helena in the heart of Napa Valley, discussing his new magazine and collectively bemoaning the state of affairs in

America's dining rooms. I come from a career grounded firmly in the hospitality industry, and my catalyst for joining the full-time ranks of wine and hospitality trainers and educators was the need to address those very real dining-room concerns, along with other industry-related challenges facing restaurants around the country.

Mark asked me to be a founding contributor to the magazine, and since *Santé*'s premiere, I haven't missed a single issue—or the opportunity to preach the gospels of customer care, product knowledge, service mechanics, and tasting skills to anyone who will listen! Eight years, hundreds of classes, and many issues later, I have been gratified, personally and professionally, to hear from so many professionals as to how these articles (or classes based in part on these articles) have impacted their lives and businesses. So in the summer of 2003, Mark and I discussed parlaying all of these pieces into a service "handbook." What follows is the result of our conversations.

A Road Map to Share

Ironically, the challenges facing operators at the time of this guide's publication are not unlike those facing the operators of the preceding decade: a challenging economy; an increasingly competitive business environment; international uncertainties contributing to a more reticent consumer state of mind; and—a surprise to nobody—rising costs in energy, labor, insurance, and raw materials. Also testing the resolve of all operators are more knowledgeable and demanding customers who are awash in so many choices and options that they can be insistent in their quest for a rewarding dining experience. And, respectfully, guests have every right to do so; they work hard for their discretionary income and should feel good about where and how they spend it. The onus is on *us* to provide value and earn their loyalty and emotional attachment.

This guide, while not a silver bullet, can be a road map for your front-of-the-house thinking. You may disagree with some of my opinions, but that's to be expected. More importantly, the opinions and approaches provide you and your coworkers with the mechanism for a healthy dialogue regarding what you do and how you do it.

In an industry that I love, I feel fortunate to have the opportunity to share my experiences with you and hope that I will continue to do so either in print or in person for years to come. In the words of John Martin, former president and CEO of Taco Bell, "If you try to save money on training, you end up spending twice as much on advertising." And, of course, we all have so much free money to spend on advertising that it is gathering dust in the corner of our offices!

Good reading, and enjoy the guide.

Evan Goldstein, MS

CUSTOMER SERVICE ★

★ ★ ★ ★

ARE YOU READY FOR TODAY'S CUSTOMERS?

The diners who come through our front doors are more knowledgeable and demanding than ever before. We must kick into high gear if we expect to satisfy them.

A surefire way to cater to and surpass the expectations of today's guests is to understand two critical contemporary points: *one*, how today's dining culture has evolved and why it's important to change with it, and *two*, who today's customers are and what motivates them. These ideas aren't complicated, but they are supercritical in today's competitive environment, and each deserves an in-depth look. Here I'll address how the restaurant industry has evolved, and next I'll cover the all-important topic of identifying and relating to today's customer.

Diners of Yesteryear

To understand the evolution of the restaurant industry, we must look to the past. In the early part of the twentieth century, the whole concept of dining out in America—putting aside beer taverns and those beloved automats—focused on fine dining. For most people fine dining was traditional, and French/European cuisine relatively expensive and limited to special occasions. As a result, people did not go out to eat as frequently as they do today. But diner demographics have changed dramatically over the years for both social and economic reasons, and diners' expectations have changed with them.

The socioeconomic influences behind shifts in dining trends start with the American family. In the past, usually the wife and/or mother did the cooking. An evening out was a celebration and a night off for Mom. Now she's bringing home the bacon, too. Cooking has become more of a hobby than a daily task. Also, our more career-focused society allows little time for cooking at home, and travel for business and pleasure has become more enmeshed in our social fabric. All of these societal changes have contributed to a stampede of hungry diners into restaurants around the country.

Dining for Dollars

Not only has time for cooking changed, but so have dining economics. A recent issue of a restaurant time-management publication reported that an average family of four saved only $6.19 by eating at home versus dining out. In 1990 it cost 93 percent more to dine out than to eat at home; in 2003 that difference dropped to 26 percent. As time has become more precious and eating out has become more affordable, dining out is no longer equated with traditional fine dining. Now it's part of day-to-day life, and this lifestyle swing has birthed a radical shift in customer expectations and modern dining culture.

So what does this mean for the restaurant industry? A lot! More than ever, diners are attracted to restaurants that offer a quick and satisfying replacement for the home-cooked meal. Of course, special-occasion restaurants will always be a top choice for important events and business dinners and for patrons with hefty bank accounts. But most of today's diner dollars originate with the "average person" looking for easy-access, quality food, served in a comfortable environment and at a good value. These dollars are also spent on more globally influenced experiences, which go beyond the classic European menu. Diners are hungry for more exotic cuisines such as Thai, Nuevo Latino, Chinese, Japanese, and creative interpretations and fusions of all of the above.

To satisfy today's customers, we need to continue to increase our understanding of the changing social and economic forces that drive their dining-out decisions. As you strategize for future success, take a hard look at your guests, and make sure your menu and dining experience meet their needs.

> More than ever, diners are attracted to restaurants that offer a quick and satisfying replacement for the home-cooked meal.

★ WHO IS TODAY'S DINER?

The largest identifiable group is, of course, the baby boomers. Born between 1946 and 1964, they're 78 million strong and possess the largest wallet full of discretionary spending dollars. Other important customers are the foodies and wine lovers who have a very acute interest in dining self-education. The third group is made up of epicurean business travelers who may be a subset of the above but will spend plenty of time and money on business and vacation travel. Members of all three groups are much sharper and more attuned, demanding, and articulate about food and beverages than ever before.

What Do Customers Want?

To cater to your core consumers, you must understand what drives them: quality, service, value, and an appetite for adventure. Today, quality is a given. Customers recognize it and won't stand for less. But remember here that improvement of quality at all levels of the industry—from ingredients to kitchen skills—has permeated every aspect of the business, from ballpark concessions to fine-dining rooms. And as the quality bar has risen, so have people's expectations.

Having better food than the guy down the block was once a competitive advantage, but food quality is now at such a high standard that service excellence has become critical to success. Superb service goes far beyond the passive experience of ordering and receiving food from a server. For the lion's share of the population, an "active" service experience—interacting with the server, shaking hands and chatting with the chef, and so forth—is what makes a meal unique and memorable. Conversely, passive service is impersonal and forgettable. To prove my point, consider what you ate during a dinner out a month ago. Unless you are a hard-core foodie, it's hard to remember, right? Now try to recall the service. Most diners are more likely to be able to describe it in detail. A good server can save a bad meal, but nothing can save a bad server.

Whether a restaurant is at the high or low end, perceived value is always clearly affected by service.

Value *at all levels of dining* is very personal and relative. What is valued by one person may be dismissed by another. But whether a restaurant is at the high or low end, perceived value is always clearly affected by service. If you spend $50 on a meal and feel as if you received a $100 experience, that's good value. If you go to an inexpensive dinner and have a miserable experience, even $20 for two feels like a rip-off. When times get tough, everyone's perspectives of value become more rigid, and the value part of the dining equation becomes even more important.

Finally, today's diners strive for adventure and are fueled by their collective experiences. This desire for discovery is spawned by travel. With airline deregulation, travel has become more affordable and accessible, and people have greater exposure to everything from regional American food to new and exciting international cuisines and wines. The influence of travel has inspired diners to want to know—and *taste*—more variety. The media is also behind this trend. For example, the Food Network has broadened the entire industry's visibility and accessibility and inspired people to explore dining rooms across the country and the globe.

Customer Satisfaction

Now that we understand who the consumer is and what he or she wants, it's easier to take a proactive role to ensure success for this year and beyond—providing we follow a few straightforward guidelines. *First,* we must become more sensitive to who our customers are and what drives them. *Second,* we should recognize that the luxury to slow down and rest on our laurels is gone forever. And *third,* we must make sure that when we have lemons (such as a sour economy or sluggish environment), we make lemonade.

Now is a good time to refine or redirect your business practices to survive in today's market. Take advantage of what you know about your business, its environment, and your customers. Leverage that knowledge against your consumer base to earn the loyalty of your present core customers and those of tomorrow.

WHAT DO DANNY MEYER, JOYCE GOLDSTEIN, AND WOLFGANG PUCK HAVE IN COMMON?

Yes, they are celebrities in the world of fine dining, but they have another commonality that you may not be aware of. They are all on record as believing that service is more important to the success of a restaurant than food. You may want to read the previous sentence again to make sure you got it right the first time. It speaks volumes about the importance of service, doesn't it?

Service is very personal. It is an interactive duet between customer and server, which can take the form of wonderful rapport, indifferent noncommunication, or out-and-out combat. Above everything else, service quality will color a diner's overall impression of the entire dining gestalt—including the food!

I have a desk covered with surveys that point to the need in our business for improved service, and there are many more out there that I haven't seen yet. One recent poll, which was conducted last July by *Zagat Survey* publisher Tim Zagat, points out that almost half of all customer complaints focused on service problems. Keep in mind that these results were compiled directly from diners—not a think tank or association.

How can you assess your current service? This may sound simplistic, but I like to walk into a restaurant and just listen to the dining "din" for a moment. I ask myself if both guests and staff are having fun, if the energy level is up, and if diners look pleased. There is a significant difference between a good restaurant "din" and a morguelike silence where people aren't enjoying themselves. Try it at other establishments and compare it with your own place. In addition, you need to dine in your own restaurant with some frequency and see it through the eyes of a customer.

Of course, you can do detailed customer research with surveys, but pressing the flesh and asking your customers how their experience was as they are leaving might provide you with information that is just as valuable, or even more so. Listen carefully to their responses, without letting your perceptions get in the way of their words. Absorb and reflect on their feedback and what you can do to address it.

Let's talk about first and last impressions, which often provide the strongest memories of a diner's experience. Ask yourself these questions:

★ If there is valet parking, is the service professional? Are uniforms clean?

★ Entering my restaurant, is the walkway clear? Is the front door free of fingerprints?

★ Are guests seated quickly and cheerfully upon arrival at the podium?

★ Are menus fresh, clean, and free of dog-eared pages?

★ Is the busser slamming bread and water on the table or landing it gently?

★ Is someone tasting the ice water and bread and butter (or oil) regularly for freshness and purity?

★ Are the restrooms and phone area checked regularly for cleanliness?

★ Is the check presented gracefully and handled quickly?

★ As guests leave, are they acknowledged? Is the door opened for them?

You get the idea here, I'm sure. All of these tiny details can create minuses for guests before they have been greeted by the server or after they have completed their meals. And keep in mind that we haven't even talked about the food! It's easier to see now why service is "more important" than food, isn't it?

They are all on record as believing that service is more important to the success of a restaurant than food.

DETAILS, DETAILS, DETAILS.

As anyone in it can tell you, the restaurant business is a detail business. Of course, the big picture is also extremely important, but when all is said and done, the details of your operation carry a disproportionate weight in the customer's mind.

Think about your last dining experience or one that a friend told you about. It easily could have sounded something like this: "I really liked the ambience, and the decor is first rate, but the bathroom looked like it hadn't been cleaned in a week, and my coffee tasted burnt." What is especially telling about this example is that the food itself didn't even make it into the description of the dining experience! When you think about what decorators and chefs cost, versus extra bathroom cleaning or a fresh pot of coffee, you can see that there is no excuse for overlooking these comparatively inexpensive elements.

I have a list of what I call my "detail barometers," elements of a restaurant's business style that separate the cream from the milk in terms of good service.

- ★ **Phone Etiquette.** Whether you are open or closed, anyone who answers the phone should be able to answer all of the basic questions about hours, directions, reservations, parking, and so on. If you have voice mail, make sure that it is simple to use and that all of those basic questions are addressed in the greeting or with a simple transfer.

  If you have a busy reservations line, make sure your reservations person asks guests if they may be placed on hold before doing so. Try to let them know how long they will be on hold, and offer to return their call instead of having them hold.

- ★ **Details at Table.** A good dining-room manager should keep a constant eye on these things, but everyone on your staff needs to be aware of them.

Make an investment in details, and keep them coming back for more.

Are table settings consistent around the table and among tables? Are silverware and glassware spotless? Have salt and pepper, sugar, and other condiments been properly wiped down? Is the menu crisp and stain free? Is the wine list in good condition? Is it an accurate listing of your stock and their correct vintages?

Is the quality of your bread, butter or olive oil, coffee, water, and desserts up to par? Taste all of them often, and if the water in your area is off tasting, add lemon slices to your water pitchers.

★ **Staff Training.** Is your staff well versed in your cuisine, preparation, and ingredients? Which dishes can be easily adjusted to meet different dietary requirements? Which ones cannot? This is an important area of knowledge that cannot be overlooked.

When your staff recites the specials, do they recite them slowly enough for guests to hear? They should always include the price of each dish. If there are more than three specials, you can do everyone a favor by printing them on the menu.

When food is delivered to the table, does the server "auction" it off? I cringe when I hear, "Now, who had the swordfish?" Need I say more?

★ **Last Impressions.** These are extremely important! Aside from server interaction during check presentation, my "detail barometers" are:
Restrooms. How often are they checked? How often are they seriously cleaned?
Coatroom. Is it secure? Can guests feel comfortable leaving their belongings there?

Now a homework assignment for you: Go through your restaurant using my "detail barometers." How would you score? Would I dine there more than once? I hope so! You spend a great deal of money to attract customers. Make an investment in details, and keep them coming back for more.

MASTERING TABLE SERVICE WILL SET YOU APART FROM THE COMPETITION.

A good portion of what I have covered in previous columns has dealt with the psychological side of service, but the mechanical components of service deserve at least as much attention. Good service mechanics are what differentiate great service from good service.

Of course, each restaurant should have a house style of service; however, there are some basics that are universal. For example, where a napkin is placed in a table setting is open to interpretation, but the placement of the knife is not. It is always placed to the right of the plate. Here are some of the other fundamentals, the "tricks," of good table service:

- ★ The cover, or table setting, should always be the same throughout the dining room, no matter who is on duty or what day of the week it happens to be.
- ★ All silverware should be burnished, and the ends of the silverware should be approximately two inches from the edge of the table. The fork is on the left; the knife is on the right with the blade facing toward the plate. Contrary to popular belief, a spoon and additional fork are only necessary if the meal being served calls for them or if you are premarking a table, as is often done in banquet service.
- ★ If there is a bread plate, it is to the left of the main plate. If a butter knife is included in the setting, it is usually situated vertically on the right side of the bread plate.
- ★ If a salad fork is being pre-set, it is placed to the left of the dinner fork so that the tips of the tines are aligned.
- ★ Napkins, as already mentioned, may be placed in a wide variety of places.
- ★ A defining moment in good service versus great service occurs with the placement of the entrée. Most of us know the rules for serving on the left and removing from the right, but how does the plate land on

Good service mechanics are what differentiate great service from good service.

the table? Karen MacNeil, cofounder of the New York Professional Service School, offers a very nice analogy. She says that the plate should be landed as if it were an airplane rather than being dropped down directly, like a helicopter. Truly phenomenal servers will determine a point on the plate that they want directly in front of the guest, place the plate on the table with this point slightly off center, and then click the plate into its proper location. You can't make the arrival of a dish much more professional-looking than this!

★ Removal of the entrée plates is another significant opportunity for great service. Many establishments do discourage removing plates before everyone at the table is done, and to be correct, no plates should be removed until everyone is finished eating. It's sad, but I see this service faux pas occurring everywhere.

★ Used silverware should be collected gently and placed on the plate before picking it up, so that it is all removed at once.

★ Scraping and stacking should never be done at table or immediately behind the guest. This can really put a sour note on an otherwise wonderful meal.

★ Some establishments use base or show plates, which are removed with the arrival of drinks or remain on the table underneath the entrée plate. Know the rules of your establishment for handling these.

★ Dessert delivery can also be scaled upward with proper plate landing and by serving any slice of cake or pie with the point toward the guest. Coffee cups should arrive on the table with the handle at the four o'clock position and with no coffee spilled in the saucer!

I hope that you will take an inventory of the techniques used by you and your establishment to see if there is room for improvement. If all of these elements are currently in use, let me know where you work. The service must be excellent!

★ IT'S SHOWTIME!

A good night out includes more than just great food and libation. We are all enormously affected by good service and presentation, which highlights the food and beverage in a way that helps diners appreciate it even more.

But before we get into the nitty-gritty, I want to state a caveat: Drama can be overdone, and when it is overdone, it is ugly. When you match your communication style to the audience and the situation, and avoid over-the-top drama, you improve your customers' dining-room experience.

A Dignified Backdrop

First, we have to set the stage. The character of the dining room should be consistent with the restaurant's concept and also one of a kind. If you want diners to take your food and wine seriously, avoid using the clichéd symbols of yesteryear—no fishing nets for seafood, no Chianti fiascos for Italian restaurants, no branding irons for steak houses.

Go for a simple, warm, elegant atmosphere. Remember, this is the stage, not the performance. And unless you want to attract a sideshow audience, avoid looking like a cheap circus. Your goal should be to achieve fine theater. My mother, who operated San Francisco's Square One for many years, always says, "The restaurant is just the envelope; the food, wine, and people are what give it personality."

With a few simple sentences, your customers feel more welcome, more part of a special experience.

Drawing the Curtain

What is the first act? It happens far from the table, when diners arrive at the restaurant, park their cars, and meet the host or hostess. Sadly, many restaurants neglect to think of their parking lots as part of the show, but they are. Even a hint of individuality in the parking lot goes a long way toward setting the tone for the evening.

I remember one establishment with a large parking lot, one that led to anxious diners racing for a spot close to the building. Rather than posting speed limits, the restaurant erected a sign that asked its customers to drive "slowly and majestically."

Opening Lines

Once inside the door, diners should be greeted and seated with grace and style. An expectant look, a small smile of recognition, and a pleasant greeting really make a difference. Why greet your diners with "How many?" or "Two?" This immediately sends the message that you view your diners as the next in line at a cattle call. God forbid the host should leave the podium and open the door for them! Imagine how that makes your guests feel on their special night out.

Instead, greet them with a friendly smile and a sincere "Good evening! How nice to see you tonight!" Please try to do this in a way that encompasses the whole group of diners. This does more than greet the customers; it also sends the message that you may remember them from a previous visit. And recognition is the first thing that makes diners feel good about a restaurant. They feel welcome and at home.

Next ask, "Do you have a reservation with us this evening?" Again, this conveys the impression that you may remember them from a previous visit. In response, they will almost always provide their name: "Yes, it's for seven. Robertson." This response allows you to respond with, "Of course, Ms. Robertson."

You are now on a personal basis with your customer. When the group is seated, take the opportunity to address the diner again: "Thank you for dining with us, Ms. Robertson. Your server will be with you in just a moment." Using people's names is a powerful and genuine way to achieve the "recognition factor," which is always tops on your guests' list of important expectations.

With a few (no more than five!) simple sentences, your customers now feel more welcome, more part of a special experience. They are ready to enjoy themselves at the kind of restaurant that treasures their business. They are happy to be here. And this is before they have even seen a menu!

IT'S SHOWTIME, ACT TWO!

The last essay offered advice on how to make guests feel special before they look at the menu—the prelude to a memorable dining experience. Now that the stage has been set and the guests are seated, let the show begin!

The Supporting Cast

Your guests should always feel like the stars of the show, but it's the wait-staff—the supporting cast—that make it happen by providing excellent service. In fact, the importance of good service cannot be overemphasized.

According to a 2002 poll by *SF Magazine* and OpenTable.com, 56 percent of customers who encounter bad service just once at an establishment said they would not return; 30 percent said they would return to a place where the service was good even if the meal was not. We are all too familiar with the adage that a great server can save a bad meal, but nothing can save a bad server!

Today's best chefs are keenly aware of the disproportionate impression that service, good or bad, makes on the guests' perception of their food. Customers seem to remember and talk about the service, good or bad, with more emotion and for a longer period of time than they do the food.

Think about it: What did you eat at XYZ Restaurant a year ago? Unless you're a foodie, most likely you will not remember. How were you treated, and how was the service? You probably still remember. Why? Because you played an active role—service is an interactive experience.

Of course, mistakes happen. But if you have a well-trained, proactive, and intuitive staff, you're more likely to maintain customer loyalty even when the kitchen or front of house commits the occasional blunder.

Basic Script and Improvisation

Excellent service is elusive—there is no one way to describe the perfect server. It is ultimately about anticipating, recognizing, and fulfilling customers' needs before they realize they have them.

But each guest's needs vary. Some diners like to feel that they're friends with their server and will encourage conversation. Others prefer that their server is neither seen nor heard but invisibly and intuitively satisfies their needs. Top waitstaff intuit what kind of a server their guests want and improvise accordingly. Here are a few basic procedures to help develop this sixth sense:

★ Start with common courtesy. Arrive at each table promptly, wait for a conversation break before greeting guests, and avoid "robotic speak" such as "Hi, my name is Evan, and I'll be your server tonight."

★ Refill near-empty breadbaskets and water or wineglasses, and clear crumbs from the table; check regularly to make sure guests have everything they need.

★ Show your team how to act with warm professionalism, good manners, and calm assuredness, and guests will know that they're in good hands.

Encore, Encore!

How do you create and sustain excellent service? An essential step is to do all you can to ensure your "supporting cast" is happy by creating a positive and supportive work environment. Good tips help keep the staff smiling, but many studies conclude that job satisfaction is more important than the almighty dollar.

Another step is to set the right example by understanding what drives your customers, which is best accomplished by regularly polling your waitstaff. Ask for qualitative feedback from your key employees, and when you get it, understand and react to their concerns. If they perceive your request for feedback as insincere, don't be surprised when the questions start coming back unanswered.

Finally, teach your waitstaff that service is a profession, not a job. You and I know that, but it is up to you to instill this notion in your staff. If you take responsibility, take charge, and take action, your staff will be happy and more effective, your customer base will be loyal and ever growing, and your business will prosper.

★ THOSE ALL-IMPORTANT FIRST AND LAST IMPRESSIONS

In my travels across the country, I have ample opportunities for evaluating dining service. In this column, I will focus on the actual server interaction and, specifically, on the first and last impressions of your customer. These are the moments that your guest will remember, so a server must pay special attention to make service memorably good.

In my experience, I find that the beginning is much more clearly defined than the conclusion. Most servers seem to make initial eye contact, possibly tell me their name, and then take a drink order or tell me about the specials. While we're on the topic, here are some tips for better first impressions:

★ Try to make your initial greeting crisp and original. If possible, move away from "Hello, my name is Bob, and I'll be your waiter this evening." Whatever you choose to say should sound as if you are saying it for the first time in your life!

★ You have only one opportunity to make a first impression. Be completely focused on your table of guests at that moment. Distracted, frazzled greetings take away from that single initial contact.

★ Recite specials comfortably, slowly enough to be understood by your guests, and please include the prices! It is always awkward for guests to have to ask about prices, so spare them that task!

★ Never touch a guest. You can be attentive and friendly without making physical contact. Of course, a handshake is the exception to this rule.

Now let's examine the end of the dining scenario, when you present the check. This is a dangerous time, when many good servers go down in flames! One mistake is what I call the "last-minute gush." You hear servers do this, and you just know it's a last-ditch effort to improve their tips. All of a sudden, the diner is their best friend, they're all grins, and the guest is not fooled for a minute. Yuck. I often encounter the obviously false "big thank you." This is also patronizing and annoying. There are better ways to make a last impression!

Think about the entire dining scenario that you have had with your guests. Something will have happened that was unique and memorable to you and your table. Perhaps there was a wine recommendation that went over especially well, a mention of a recent sporting event, or a dish that was successfully adjusted to the diner's request. Take one of these "events" and use it in your final closing moment. For example, you could conclude your interaction by saying something like, "I'm glad that you liked the Clos du Bois Alexander Valley Reserve Cabernet Sauvignon so much. Next time you visit us, I have another wonderful Cabernet Sauvignon for you to try."

These final words acknowledge that you have been paying attention to your customers and that their satisfaction is important to you. You can thread any positive or amusing part of your interaction with them into your closing. (Please note that if your guests are dining with children, you get extra points for recalling something involving them. Parents love this.)

It may sound almost too easy, but believe me, it works. Don't be surprised when these guests ask for one of your tables the next time they come to your restaurant! And you get extra bonus points if, when they return, you can recall something that happened during their last visit. "Would you like to try the Cabernet Sauvignon I mentioned during your last visit? We're featuring it tonight by the glass."

Try working on those first and last impressions and watch your service (and tips) improve!

The end of the dining scenario is a
    dangerous time, when many good servers
        go down in flames.

COMPLAINTS SHOULD ALWAYS BE MET WITH GRATITUDE.

I am always grateful when a customer takes the time to tell me about his or her experience and gives us the chance to make up for any mistakes that we may have made. After all, most unhappy guests say nothing—they simply don't come back. And they may tell all their friends!

As I listen carefully to my clientele, I apply one of my favorite rules: Perception is reality. If your customers believe that something is true, then it *is* true in their eyes. I also know that for every customer who cares enough to voice a complaint, there are ten more who feel the same way but haven't bothered to tell us. If that isn't enough to keep you awake at night . . .

> ## Perception is reality. If your customers believe that something is true, then it *is* true in their eyes.

There are some standard complaints that come up frequently, but in our myopia, we tend to overlook the obvious. Here are a few diners' pet peeves that regularly appear on the various Internet wine and food message boards.

- ★ **The wineglasses are inadequate.** When diners order a $40 bottle of wine, they hate to have it served in $1 glasses. Even if diners don't complain out loud, they are unhappy. Trust me. You should serve your best wines in a glass that has an ample bowl, a thin rim, and an elegant stem. In the words of celebrated restaurateur Leonce Picot, "Buy the best glassware that you can afford, given the practicalities of your establishment."
- ★ **The wineglasses are overfilled.** Never fill the glasses more than half full to allow diners to swirl the wine a bit in the glass and to appreciate the bouquet. If you overfill, you are depriving your customers of their right to fully enjoy the wine, and you are telling them that you don't

know any better. They may conclude that you are just trying to finish off the bottle so that you can sell them another one.

The one exception to this rule is the by-the-glass pour; select a glass that allows for a two-thirds pour but is consistent with pouring cost. Believe me, customers care about this.

★ **The staff is not educated.** If the server doesn't know the answers to questions about the food and wine, how are customers supposed to make the right choices? Your guests may not agree with the server's opinion, but they do expect a server to know and care about the food and wine in your restaurant. All too often, servers seem more interested in selling food or drinks than in enhancing the guest's dining experience. This strategy may work once, but that customer won't come back.

★ **The dining room is too dark.** No, bright lights don't make for a restful and romantic atmosphere, but all too often, I hear from people who can't read the menu because the lights are too low. Remember, many of our best customers are a bit older, with diminished eyesight. That delicate, elegant script may look good in the design studio, but make sure that it can be read by candlelight by patrons in their sixties.

★ **The dining room is too loud.** As with lighting, sound can be a generational issue. Younger people tend to like or to endure more noise than older people, so make sure that your "white noise" (music, conversation and kitchen sounds) level isn't driving away half your customers. Many older people use hearing aids or have trouble hearing, and background noise makes table conversation much more difficult. While young people may be more willing to stare wordlessly into each other's eyes, most older folks think of pleasant conversation as a key element to a nice dinner. Don't chase them away.

Would you dine in a restaurant where you are served wine in cheap, over-filled glasses; can't read the menu or hear each other talk; and have to instruct the server at every step? Neither would I. If any one of these problems arose, I might bring it to the attention of the manager. Which is what I hope I am doing right now!

★ WORD-OF-MOUTH REFERRALS ARE IMPORTANT.

Happy customers who enjoy the service, ambience, food, and beverage at your restaurant will tell their friends about it. On the flip side, consumer research tells us that a dissatisfied customer is 11 times more likely to tell people about a bad restaurant experience. In our business, customer dissatisfaction is a supercritical issue.

In training your staff to handle problems, I think it's important to view complaint handling as an investment in future business. When a complaint is voiced, you and your team should be grateful. Most unhappy people out there just fume quietly, leave the restaurant, complain to their friends, and never return. At least when someone vocalizes a grievance, you get a chance to turn a negative into a positive.

★ **Reacting to Complaints.** How should we react to a complaint? The single most important element is quality listening: being fully focused, making good eye contact, and not being distracted by the chaos that might be surrounding you. Along with listening well, you must create a sense of empathy. Nod as you listen to the problem, ask questions if appropriate, and then repeat the problem back to the customer to make sure that you understand the situation completely. Let your guest know that you are in his or her corner.

As you become better at listening and empathizing, you will find that many people need just that. Once they have "vented," they are likely to feel better about the problem. All you need to do is tell them that their complaint will be addressed and, if possible, how it will be addressed.

Last, but certainly not least, an apology is in order. The challenge is to apologize without assigning blame to anyone. You may want to blame someone with all your might, but don't do it! The apology will come off as insincere and unprofessional. Your customer does not

View complaint handling as an investment in future business.

need to know exactly where the service or food preparation chain broke down. All he or she really wants to know is that you care, that your establishment cares, and that something will be done to resolve the issue.

★ **Restaurant Policies.** Your restaurant may have policies for responding to complaints. If such policies exist, review them carefully to make sure that they are accomplishing the intended goal. Restaurants often have a "comp" policy, but I strongly recommend using freebies only when appropriate. For example, if a party is kept waiting 45 minutes for their table in the bar area, sending them an appetizer and sincere regrets might be appropriate. If the complaint is that they have waited too long for their check, keeping them at the restaurant with a complimentary after-dinner drink or dessert does not achieve the goal.

★ **Resolving Complaints.** In many cases, a resolution to a complaint is obvious—but not always. When appropriate, I recommend asking the customer exactly what would make him or her happy. I know that restaurateurs sometimes hesitate to do this, expecting that the customer will ask for full ownership of their establishment, but this really doesn't happen! If you've done a good job listening and empathizing, you have nothing to fear. A great training technique is role playing. You can use complaints that have surfaced recently as examples.

If you're not yet sold on the value of handling complaints effectively, then consider this: If customers were choosing between a new, unknown restaurant and your establishment and, during their last visit, you handled a problem to their satisfaction, where do you think they would dine? If you played your cards right, they would be headed to your place!

FEW OCCUPATIONS ARE AS STRESSFUL AS BEING A SERVER.

While they often enjoy good pay, flexible hours, and delicious food, one thing servers do not enjoy is confronting a customer over a difficult situation. Here are my thoughts on handling two of these stress-filled trials.

Reservation Resolution

How should you handle customers who swear that they have a reservation, even though their names are not in your book?

★ Approach the matter as a problem that you both share and that you both would like to resolve. The first rule of etiquette is to avoid being combative or defensive. After all, unhappy customers are likely to tell 22 other people about it, while happy ones tell only eight. Those are lousy odds.

★ Immediately gather as much information as you can from the customers. You may discover that either your host or the guests made a mistake about the time, day, or even week or month.

★ Resolve the conflict quickly and effectively. Let the customer know that you are concerned about the problem and are trying to come up with a solution. Make eye contact and be emphatic. Try to accommodate the party at the bar or squeeze in another table.

★ Take into account your other guests, too. Finding a table for these guests at 6:30 may be fine, but not if it means that your 7:30 guests have reservations and no table. Always keep the discussion polite, helpful, and positive. This is where your mastery of your profession can turn a difficult situation into a tour de force!

★ Reward your unhappy guests for their patience. You are far better off providing the customers with a complimentary bottle of Champagne at the bar than you are fighting their anger for the rest of the night and beyond. Remember, your guests may not always be right, but they are always customers.

Credit Card Conflicts

Here's another stressful moment: the dreaded declined credit card.

★ Submit the card again. Only if a card is declined a second time should you approach the customer with the news.

★ Invite the guest to discuss the matter away from his or her table. This is an embarrassing spot for anyone, so simply ask the customer to join you at the podium, away from the attention of his or her guests.

★ Be diplomatic and polite. Convey, both in your words and in your body language, that you sympathize with your guest and are interested in resolving this dilemma as quickly and considerately as possible.

★ Don't blame the customer. Use phrases such as, "Sorry for the inconvenience. We are having difficulties processing this credit card," rather than the more direct and personal, "The card that you gave me was rejected."

★ Suggest an alternative method of payment. Another card, a check, or cash might be easier, quicker, and more convenient for the customer.

★ Deal with a bad credit card carefully. If you have been notified by the credit card company that the rejected card should be destroyed, phone the credit card company directly to discuss the matter and to make sure that there is no mistake. Then invite the customer to join you at the podium, where he or she can speak to the company directly. By standing nearby during this conversation, you can offer help when needed, and you can also read the body language of your guest. It will become obvious if you need to hold the card.

The two scenarios above are enough to give a pang of worry to any server, but the solutions are simple. Work politely with your guests to resolve the issue. In the long run, most people will be grateful for your tactful resolution of a problem that they find equally stressful.

Remember, your guests may not always be
right, but they are always customers.

★ CUSTOMERS WE LOVE TO HATE.

It's not often that we think of the Wild West as a place to contemplate top-level service, but a visit to a Northern California ghost town gave me a great idea. Walking into an abandoned saloon, I noticed a large sign on the wall that said, "Gentlemen, Please Check Your Guns with the Bartender." While I stood contemplating whether the sign was authentic, a series of loud beeps from a fellow tourist's cell phone startled me, and a brainstorm erupted: Wouldn't it be great if we could post a big sign on our front doors that states emphatically, "Ladies and Gentlemen, Please Check Your Cell Phones with the Hostess"? We could have another one that says, "Please Check Your Screaming Toddlers with the Maître d'" and another one imploring, "Please Don't Break off Your Engagement in Our Restaurant." And another . . . Well, you get the idea.

Curbing Disturbing Behavior

Most diners understand what kinds of behaviors are appropriate in restaurants. Unfortunately, others don't know, or they forget. How can we keep them from creating disturbances that can ruin the evening for everyone else? Remember that we are always supposed to provide solutions and options as part of our job. Here are some suggestions.

★ **Cell phones.** Managing behavior is easier when you state your policy up front. For cell phones, an ounce of prevention is worth a pound of cure. While I wouldn't suggest a sign at the door, I do advocate a discreet note on the menu, something like, "This restaurant is a quiet haven from the stress and tumult of everyday life. Please help us by turning off your cell phone while dining here."

Let's not assume this notice will be completely effective. What should you do when a diner's phone rings?

I would immediately approach the table and suggest that the diner step into an office where he or she could have more privacy. This gesture not only removes the cell phone from the dining room but also sends a nice message to nearby tables that you are trying your best to provide them with the kind of experience they expect.

When the diner finishes the call, you could then call his or her attention to the notice on the menu. Of course, one needs to balance this policy against a dining couple's anticipated call from a baby-sitter or on some other matter of importance. Asking these guests to use the vibrate function in lieu of a beep is a feasible compromise, or you could provide them with the number of your restaurant's phone.

★ **Screaming children.** You can't advise against this behavior on the menu! No parents want their children to misbehave, but if it happens, you can stop by the table and offer assistance. And while I will never forget the lovely owner of a Japanese restaurant who once carried our daughter around for 35 minutes while we ate our dinner, I don't think it is our job to baby-sit unruly kids.

You can, however, offer a quiet room where the parent can take the child and provide any food or drink that might help quiet the child. I can't count the number of times I have donated my office during dining hours for just this purpose. This solution has the added benefit of building a great relationship with the parents—they will return, again and again. You should never overlook playing to the kids, no matter what their age.

★ **Diners who choose your restaurant to end their engagement.** Sorry, this is a problem for which I can offer no surefire solution. Before jumping into the middle of a lovers' scrum to restore peace, remember that something like half of all police fatalities involve domestic disputes! My suggestion? Keep your distance and your other customers out of range as much as possible—and maybe wear a bulletproof tastevin.

"Ladies and Gentlemen, Please Check Your Cell Phones with the Hostess."

MARKETING

★ WHAT MAKES *YOU* SO SPECIAL?

Many of us take the basic kinds of restaurant promotions for granted, but it is naive to assume that marketing doesn't need the same attention to detail as your service and food preparation.

The best way to generate more customers is to make sure that your current customers are so happy that they will return again and bring their friends, family, and business associates. Studies suggest that it is five times more expensive to attract a new customer than it is to keep an existing one, so make it your mission to keep the captive audience content!

Restaurant marketing, however, is a lot more complex than keeping your customers satisfied. You need to first define your establishment in terms of the competition, and then present that finding in an effective way to your target market. In short, restaurant marketing means answering the question, "What makes you so special?" and then ensuring that your target audience knows the answer, too.

> Look for the things that make you unique and interesting to your customers.

Market Analysis

What kind of restaurant are you? Marketers use a standard Strengths/Weaknesses/Opportunities/Threats analysis to help them answer this question. List the attributes of those four categories for your restaurant and compare them to your competition. Look for the things that make you unique and interesting to your customers. That's your market positioning—who you are and what makes you different.

Your analysis may conclude that you are not unique in your market, in which case your challenge is to take a look at what you do and to find ways to distinguish yourself from the other area restaurants. Better service, valet parking, more interesting wines, more innovative menus, and specific themes are all ways that you can draw a distinction between your restaurant and the competition.

What approach is best for you? That depends on your business goals and your local market. Look at the big picture, think for the long term, and steer your course to a unique position.

Eye on the Target

The first step is easy: look around. Take a walk that covers a five-block radius from your restaurant. This is your best potential market. Why are people here, what do they do, and where do they go? If you can answer these questions, then you can fine tune your restaurant to their interests.

★ **Are you in the heart of the business district?** Consider lunch business. Call on the companies in your vicinity and set up accounts to make their business lunches as convenient as possible. Get to know the key players at each business and treat them like royalty. A broadcast fax with your specials each week is a great way to keep your name in front of them.

★ **Are you a neighborhood restaurant?** Look to local community papers for coverage. Your support of a neighborhood charity might do a lot more for your business than joining 20 other restaurants in a regional promotion. Learn about the area residents and find ways to get them involved in your restaurant, from promotions and events to menu selections and specials.

★ **Are you in a tourist area?** Working with hotel concierges may be the best marketing ploy of all. They can send you more business than anyone else in town, and they should be treated accordingly. Invite them to the restaurant, thank them for their referrals, make sure that they know all about you, and give every one of their referrals an experience to remember.

Don't forget your staff—your most important audience. Your training programs should cover marketing concepts, and you and your staff should always be looking for ways to enhance your restaurant's image.

Marketing a restaurant requires focused thought and energy and a basic plan that everyone understands, from the new busboy to your most distinguished customer. And it requires you to pay attention to every detail.

So what's new?

YOU CAN'T DO TOO MUCH FOR YOUR BEST CUSTOMERS.

When Square One opened in San Francisco nearly 17 years ago, I knew even then that our most important market was located within six blocks of the restaurant. We were, after all, the local restaurant for this audience, and we never wanted to give them a reason to go farther afield. I called it our home-field advantage.

That marketing approach is true for any restaurant, not just Square One. Whether they are located within six blocks or farther than 600 miles, your core customers are vital to the success of your enterprise.

Rewarding Loyalty

We worked diligently to take care of those local "friends of the restaurant." We squeezed them in where and when we could, even when they arrived without a reservation. We faxed them copies of our menus to tempt them with our daily specials. We remembered what they liked and how they liked it. In turn, they became loyal customers, good friends, and walking sandwich boards for us.

When it comes right down to it, we really are talking about more than a normal business relationship, and that is as it should be. Normal business relationships may work well for some industries, but not for restaurants. Providing food to people is a very nurturing, loving, and personal business! If we do our job right and go beyond a basic business relationship with our customers, we will be rewarded. Clients will respond on both a business and a personal, even an emotional level. That personal level is the foundation of a much closer relationship with your customers and of long-term loyalty, a primary goal of any establishment.

Once, when we heard that one of our best customers was in the hospital, we sent him flowers. He called to thank us for the flowers, and during that conversation, he bemoaned the quality of the food that he was being served at the hospital. We knew just what to do. We hired a cab and delivered several of his favorite dishes directly to his room. He was the most loyal of customers one could ever wish for, and even today, with the restaurant no longer with us, he is still a good friend. This may have been an unusual circumstance, but it was also an opportunity to make a lasting impression with a great customer. And that is what great service is all about.

Whether it be for health reasons or just tight scheduling, your best customers may not always be able to get to your restaurant. They may love you, but between business, family, and their other interests, it may be hard for them to come in to the restaurant as often as they would like. Do you want to lose that business when there is a way to keep it?

The Extra Mile

Under the circumstances, a restaurant should go the extra mile to get the food to the customer. On occasion at Square One, we delivered key lunches to local offices, prepared dinners for nearby businesspeople to pick up on their way home, and created appetizer assortments for our customers' dinner parties. We went out of our way to make them happy and, along the way, generated extra business. After all, these were our customers, and we did not want them to become somebody else's.

Yes, our approach was a bit unusual. Yes, it was a bit more work for the kitchen. Other restaurants were unwilling to do the same, which was exactly why we did it. We were willing to do that little bit extra for our customers. They remembered that many months and even years later, and they appreciated our effort. I know, because even though Square One is closed, they still tell me about it!

If we do our job right and go beyond a basic business relationship with our customers, we will be rewarded.

WHAT SETS THE BEST RESTAURANTS APART?

People return to restaurants for a number of reasons, among them recognition, ambience, service, and, in fourth position, food and beverage. This surprises a lot of people, but not me. Most restaurants offer good food and beverages these days, if you are not providing quality, people simply won't return.

What elevates a restaurant above the also-rans is a unique experience. It's what I refer to as that last ten percent. You have to exceed to succeed.

One very good way of distinguishing yourself from the crowd is to turn your restaurant into a wine destination. Fortunately, you don't have to have a wine list with 16,000 wines or a complete vertical of Château Margaux back to the turn of the century to draw wine enthusiasts, but it does require work and a simple objective—to encourage wine-loving diners to think of you first. Here are some suggestions for achieving that goal.

★ **Start by creating a sense of drama about wine.** Large bottles in your reception area give your customers an immediate and elegant sense of your commitment to fine wine. Earn extra mileage from these bottles by promoting special-event dinners where such bottles are opened and served alongside a series of specially paired courses. If these wines are one-of-a-kind lots purchased at auction or exclusive, private-label bottlings, the message will be even stronger.

★ **Pre-set each table with nice wineglasses.** Good stemware tells your guests that you know and care about wine and that their wine selections will be given the attention and service that they deserve. With an unspoken act of service, wine is now on their radar screen.

★ **Use the fine-wine theme as an element in your dining-room décor.** From framed wine posters and wooden case ends to towering glass wine cellars, wine is a decorating theme that creates ambience and sends a positive message to your clientele.

★ **Match your wine list to your restaurant.** The wines should work well with

One very good way of distinguishing yourself from the crowd is to turn your restaurant into a wine destination.

and be priced in line with the menu. Check your pricing and corkage charges against your competition. If you are aggressive here, guests will notice your interest and dedication.

★ **Offer a depth of wines from a region or of a particular style.** This approach creates excitement and will encourage your guests to return to try something different. By focusing your wine list, you will quickly attract aficionados of those wines.

★ **Create an ambitious wine-by-the-glass program.** It can work its magic, allowing diners who might be hesitant to purchase an unfamiliar bottle to try two or three wines and to learn as they enjoy them. Expand this by-the-glass concept by offering flights of wines to compare or diverse selections of half glasses.

★ **Plan menu-pairing dinners to showcase your special wines.** Many wineries promote such dinners when their winemakers are in town, and wine societies are often looking for a restaurant that will host their meetings and events. If you want to be a wine destination restaurant, you should explore these opportunities enthusiastically.

★ **Fire up your staff and train them well.** If you offer new and interesting wines each month, your staff must be trained to keep up. Make sure that you have the staff taste new wines so that they understand how the wines work with the dishes on your menu.

If you can create a reputation for your restaurant as the local fine-wine focus, you also can travel far toward another goal. As you and the staff share your enthusiasm and knowledge of wines with your customers, your guests will respond in kind. The relationship with your clientele will evolve in depth and interest, and you will begin to pull ahead of the competition in those other critical areas of restaurant performance: recognition, ambience, and service.

You will exceed your competition and succeed in your market.

★ HOW MANY WAYS CAN YOU SAY, "MAY I HELP YOU?"

I've talked about going that extra mile to help your customers, even when they can't visit your restaurant. Here I'll touch on some of the many innovative approaches to reach your customers.

Time-Sensitive Service

Take-out food is a great way to make a lasting impression on your present and future clientele, but there is more to it than just making a good impression. Of course, many "ethnic" restaurants have been taking advantage of the take-out concept for years. From pad thai to pizza, from tacos to tandoori, many establishments have learned that they can increase sales beyond the capacity of their dining room by offering food to go and/or for delivery. Should you do the same?

Anything that provides value to the customer is worth considering. Right now, the most valuable commodity that your customers have is time; they don't have enough of it, and they don't want to spend it on details. If you can make your restaurant "easier" and more accessible to your customers, you should certainly try to do so.

> Anything that provides value to the customer is worth considering.

By the way, many of your suppliers are going the extra mile to make your life easier, too. Many now have Web sites that give you all the necessary information to use and promote their products successfully. For example, Allied Domecq Wines USA has an informational Web site, www.allied-domecqwines.com, that provides everything you need for your wine list, from technical information about the wines to tasting notes, and if you're a trade registrant, access to other e-tools. Without question, this is the wave of the future, because it serves the customer!

In addition, new companies have sprung up, willing to take an order on the phone or by fax, pick up the food at the restaurant, and deliver it to the customer's home. As those companies grow in importance, you should make every effort to ensure that your customers don't have any reason to leave you for other restaurants.

E-Commerce and Extras

Takeout/delivery is only the tip of the iceberg. Good restaurants are now creating Web sites and posting their menus on the Internet. The on-line menus not only tempt customers with delicious options but also help them decide what to order and where. In some cases, they can call ahead, place their order, and know that it will be ready when they arrive. And they won't miss Act One of *Tosca*.

Other restaurants have found that their retail customers love certain dishes or condiments. The smart ones have created a new branch of their business just to make sure that their customers remain satisfied. At the same time, they are developing a valuable "brand awareness" for their restaurant—one that reaches well outside the dining room.

While barbecue joints have often sold their sauce on the side, this retailing avenue is now a source of revenue and a way of serving customers at some of the most famous restaurants in America. Alice Waters sells her wonderful granola by the pound. Seafood restaurants sell their "clambake to go," Indian restaurants sell their chutneys, and grills sell their famous sausages. In fact, now you can buy an entire lobster dinner from Legal Seafoods, all delivered to your home inside its own cooking pot. Bob Dylan was right—"the times they are a-changin'"!

All of this serves a great purpose. Yes, money is made, but that is often a by-product of the real rationale. To develop rewarding, long-term relationships with their customers, restaurants have developed new reasons for people to call, visit, and do business with them.

And that is good service, any way you look at it.

TRENDS MEAN CHANGE—FOR THE BETTER!

As an ex-restaurateur, I always felt that we had to walk a fine line between creating our own identity and responding to the trends in the marketplace. In a worst-case scenario, one has a traditional Mediterranean meal with a Monday-night football promotion, featuring little pigskin "dim sum"! In a best case, however, your restaurant can use the trends of today to provide even better service to your customers, and that's the secret to success.

Special Sampler Menus

Certainly, one opportunity that should be addressed is the trend for more sampler-type menus. These menus offer your customers a chance to taste a number of dishes, whether they be simply a special combination platter of appetizers or a more evolved concept that covers an entire dinner.

At Gary Danko's eponymous restaurant in San Francisco, customers are offered a prix fixe menu that allows them to choose anything from appetizers through dessert. The cost of the meal is computed only by the number of courses—two, three, four, and so on. Guests can order what they want and how much they want, creating their own "cook's tour" with the help of the service staff. On top of that, from this selection palette, the restaurant orchestrates the order. It doesn't matter if you pick three from the appetizer or entrée segments; they can and will make it work.

Adding Wine to the Menu

Please don't stop with the food. Because each course is an opportunity for you to offer a new taste to your customers, it is also a chance for you to show off your wine selections and expertise.

In Europe, the traditional prix fixe menu very well may include a glass of the beverage of your choice. Why not make this sampler menu truly memorable and include in the price a sampler selection of small "taster portions" of two to four wines to accompany your meal? Or if wines are not part of the

You can offer your customers new and interesting experiences, and in some ways, that's the name of the game.

sampler-menu deal, why not offer them via a supplemental charge? Or let your waiter/sommelier customize a series of wines by the glass or even half-bottles tailored to the specific choices.

In and Out

Some restaurants even take this "customized menu" approach to the next level, offering a table in the kitchen where diners can not only watch the preparation of the food but also chat with the kitchen staff about everything from sauces and spices to portion size and timing. Here is the ultimate behind-the-scenes look at food while it is being created, and it's also a personal and special experience for both you and your guests.

An opposite trend is the recent boom in take-out orders, where diners barely set foot in the restaurant but order everything from a few appetizers to a full-blown meal. It's a fascinating development and one worthy of attention.

Of course, special menus work much better if you have trained your staff to take full advantage of the food and wine opportunities. Simply serving the wines with the food will not do. Your staff should be well versed in the philosophy of wine and food matching, and they should use the unique menu offerings to share some of those thoughts with your diners.

What's the point of all this? At the very least, you can offer your customers new and interesting experiences, and in some ways, that's the name of the game. In addition, you give your staff a new way to develop a strong relationship with your guests. You may even provide patrons with a new way to think about wine and food—something that they will remember for the rest of their lives. After all, that is exactly what we are trying to do each and every night that we open for business.

★ WHAT'S THE MOST VALUABLE PIECE OF RESTAURANT EQUIPMENT YOU OWN?

While you may think it is the walk-in or your new stove, I would like to suggest that it's something a littler simpler—the telephone. Indirectly, nothing in your restaurant can cost you or make you more money or attract more customers. For the front of the house, the telephone is your only direct link to potential customers. That link, and your ability to use it, should never be taken for granted.

A Profit-Making Detail

An employee with good phone manners can play a key role in selling your restaurant. How? A telephone "maestro" can direct your customers to visit at hours that are more convenient to you, encourage them to try your restaurant for the first time, and point out specialties of the house—all gestures that contribute directly to the bottom line. On a more subjective note, good telephone manners are one of the great distinguishing details of any restaurant, right up there with valet parking, top-quality coffee, good bread, and fabulous desserts.

Details are what ultimately help make your reputation and your restaurant stand out from the crowd, and details have a disproportionately important impact on your guests. In some ways, the telephone is the most important of these. After all, the telephone is often your customers' first impression. Long before they arrive at your door, use the valet parking, or meet the maître d', they are judging your restaurant by their phone conversation with you.

Telephone Tips

Here are nine quick tips to help you handle the telephone and make it work for you.

1. In a world of voice mail, a live person answering the telephone makes a difference. Or are you too busy to talk to your customers?
2. If you must use a voice-mail system, make the opening menu user

Long before customers arrive at your door, they are judging your restaurant by their phone conversation with you.

friendly. Make sure that the first option they have is to talk to someone about making or changing a reservation.

3. Never let the phone ring more than three times. If it does, either you are ignoring your customers or you are incompetent. That's a terrible message to send over the phone.

4. Greet your phone guests cordially and graciously, both in language and in tone. Remember, you are still on stage, even if you can't see the audience. Be cordial and professional and never laugh at a request.

5. Develop a simple, one-page telephone script that will answer your customers' basic questions—directions, prices, hours, dress code, etc. Answer the phone with "Good afternoon" or "Good morning," and follow that with the name of the restaurant. When you are done, thank them for calling, and do it by name, always using Mr., Mrs., or Ms.

6. Take the time to repeat all of the reservation information back to the caller. They will confirm the date, time, and number in the party and will correct any mistakes that either of you have made.

7. Try not to put your customers on hold, but if you must, ask them first and wait for their OK. Also, let them know how long you'll be; if it is more than 30 seconds, offer to call them back. The alternative is to leave them hanging. They may get tired of waiting and hang up, which means that you will never hear about their canceled reservation, their birthday party, or their special request.

8. Always be gracious, even when guests are calling to cancel a reservation or to change the time or number in their party. After all, they called to let you know, which is better than not calling at all. Thank them for their courtesy.

9. Never promise on the phone what you can't deliver in person. Remember that your goal is to define the customer's expectation, then meet it. Your ability to accomplish that will have a great bearing on your success as a restaurant.

AT TAX TIME, PRACTICE "COMPASSIONATE OPPORTUNISM."

The month of April conjures up pleasant thoughts of springtime bloom and the promise of brighter days and warmer weather. But sunny visions can't always bleach out the dark shadow of tax time. For the restaurant industry, mid-April can be an especially tough period, when business often dips and anxiety runs high. On the flip side, tax time offers opportunities to create special programs and promotions that help boost business, customer loyalty, and staff and client morale. So set aside your calculator and mountain of receipts and consider the following ways to take the "taxing" out of tax season.

★ **Exercise a little more TLC with guests and staff.** Around April 15, many taxpayers are feeling the stress of the season and tightening their discretionary spending. Talk to your staff and prepare them for a lean April, when traffic and tips are likely to be lower and patrons' anxiety higher. Encourage them to be compassionate and, if possible, to refer to customers by name. People are often down during tax time, and a little creature comfort through name recognition makes them feel better.

★ **Steer your guests toward midpriced menu items and beverages.** Playing down high-ticket selections is another subtle but demonstrative way of expressing empathy and having your customers feel better about their purchases.

★ **On a positive note, pushing less-expensive items often results in larger sales.** If you sell a $25 bottle of Sauvignon Blanc rather than a $35 bottle of Chardonnay, your customers may feel they have the financial flexibility to order a second bottle. Share these thoughts with your staff so they can anticipate and support your guests' desires and pursue a strategy that may lead to increased sales—and higher tips.

★ **Build budget-friendly menu packages.** Offering more comfort foods, less-expensive entrée options, or more "shared" plate appetizers are tangible ways to display your compassion. Smaller dishes and global tapas, specially priced appetizers, or desserts paired specifically with selected glasses or half-glasses of wine are other means of demonstrating perceived value. The more "deals" you offer on your menu, the more attractive it will be when patrons are feeling the IRS pinch.

★ **Turn up your tax-time promotions.** When you have lemons, make lemonade! Tax-time thematic meals and promotions tell guests you're rewarding them while Uncle Sam is taking a bite out of their paycheck. Create and promote a "chase away that tax-time blues" type of happy hour with $4.15 cocktails of proprietary blended-spirits drinks and appetizer specials with appropriate-for-the-season catchy names, or sprinkle similarly priced promotional items throughout your menu. For evenings you anticipate will be slow, create special events specific to tax time. Publicize a well-priced prix fixe dinner with wine and stage it for an early or late seating. Besides offering good deals to your stressed-and-strapped guests, you are showing your compassion for their plight.

★ **Create added convenience.** For customers too tied up in tax preparation to indulge in a leisurely lunch, implement tax-time take-out menus. Better yet, offer delivery for accounting firms or others who may be strapped down during this period. This ploy is a fantastic way to reward loyal customers and an effective way to introduce new diners to your enterprise.

★ **Power up your promotions.** Don't expect your clientele to learn about your specials on their own—it's your job to get the word out. Target your mailing list, local businesses, and your local newspaper's food section for your special events and offerings.

Now that you're prepared to make the most of an otherwise slow period, don't forget to give yourself some slack, too. And remember: Show your customers you care. After the stress of tax season is behind them, they'll return to celebrate!

Talk to your staff and prepare them for a lean April, when traffic and tips are likely to be lower and patrons' anxiety higher.

HUMAN RESOURCES ★★★

WHAT IS THE NUMBER ONE ISSUE FACING RESTAURATEURS?

I am sure that everyone in our business can answer this question without thinking. It's attracting and keeping qualified staff. I need not point out the countless local and national restaurant association surveys or the myriad conference seminars on the subject that validate this concern. The recent dip in the economy notwithstanding, thousands of new restaurants have opened in the past few years and have endured. It feels as if the doors on our restaurants are revolving only to take care of the staff turnover!

So what can you do to make your life easier? The answer may not be obvious, because the best way to make your life easier is to work harder. You have to invest in your staff the same way you invest in your wine cellar, dining room, or advertising. In my opinion, great employees are not born; they are trained. You have to invest time, money, and energy in your staff every day. Here we'll address investing time.

Spending Time Saves Time

Doesn't it seem ironic that the best way to reduce your workload is to increase the time you spend with your staff? The more training and education you provide, the more they can manage without you. That's a good thing, but it's a simple equation that many managers frequently forget.

There is almost no chance that the person applying for a job in your restaurant will have all the qualifications needed to do the job perfectly. Many of my friends have come to realize that simply teaching servers the difference between Chardonnay and Cabernet is more the norm than the exception in this labor-challenged environment. You have to expect that every new employee will require training on every element of the job, from customer contact to kitchen logistics. If you are not doing that training, you are creating big problems for yourself.

Don Fletcher, a very successful restaurateur in Auckland and president of the New Zealand Restaurant Association, once told me, "If you have an employee who doesn't seem to be working out, the first question you should

Great employees are not born;
they are trained. You have to invest time,
money, and energy in your staff every day.

ask is, 'Have I given this employee all the training that [he or she] needs to do the job well?'" If the answer is no, don't look beyond the mirror for the solution to the problem.

Every service employee at your restaurant should be trained and educated on the basics of every service function. They should know more than just how you do it; they should know why you do it, as well. They should buy into your system, so that they can do it with style and enthusiasm. Your job is to convey that essence to them.

Spending Time Saves Staff

If you train your staff well, you will accomplish at least two very important goals: You will have given your employees the tools that they need to make your restaurant successful, and you will have made your life easier. There is another benefit, as well: You will give your employees a reason to stay with you.

Training isn't just a once-in-a-lifetime class; it is a long-term experience. If you make that true at your restaurant, then the longer those employees stay with you, the more they will learn—and the more reason they will have to stay.

Of course, many people in our business resist training their staffs completely for fear that such highly trained employees might leave. I always find that tragically funny. On the one hand, I can have a terrific staff that is so well trained that my competitors are trying to steal them. On the other hand, I may lose my best-trained employees.

Which would you prefer—to have highly trained employees leave your restaurant, spreading the good word about the quality and quantity of your staff training, or to have your poorly trained staff stay in their positions for the rest of their lives? The answer is pretty obvious, isn't it?

DO YOU HAVE A WINNING TEAM?

There was a time when jobs were specialized, even in the restaurant business. The front of the house was one "job," and the back of the house "job" was altogether different. Bussers never poured wine, waiters rarely cleared plates, and sommeliers never looked at the water glasses, much less filled them.

Those days are over. Today, great service depends on a team approach, where every player not only understands his or her own responsibilities but also everyone else's. Seeing the restaurant through the eyes of your guests is the norm, and "it's not my job" is a phrase that should never be heard. Your staff may be asked to plate and portion desserts, make coffee, and do whatever else it takes to make things work.

How do you train your staff to think as a team? Here are a few tips to help convince them to buy into the new on-premises reality and ensure that they are on the side of both you and your customers.

- ★ **Offer financial incentives that reward everyone for doing a good job.** Make these perks inclusive, not exclusive, and you will find that the entire staff will pay attention to your customers' needs. Incentive programs in which the same people win all the time are not productive; the nonwinners will cease to participate.
- ★ **Institute a staff-education program that goes beyond job basics.** Does your training cover company philosophy and a general overview of all the jobs in the dining room? Do you talk about the customer as the focus of attention?
- ★ **Include everyone in wine service and tasting training.** If you feel that wine training is not for everyone, what message are you sending to those you exclude? You are telling them that when it comes to wine, they should not care and they should not get involved.

    That's a big mistake, because so much of the team effort and team approach depends on everyone's feeling involved in the process. Your

> Today, great service depends on a team approach, where every player not only understands his or her own responsibilities but also everyone else's.

training is incomplete unless every staff member, including those in the kitchen, can talk knowledgeably about the food and drink that you offer.

★ **Tell your staff when they do a good job and when they have worked hard.** All too often, I find service staff receiving more positive reinforcement from the customers than from the restaurant management. While it's important that they are making the customer happy, never let them get the impression that you don't appreciate their efforts. In these days of limited labor pools, praise for good work may prevent your best staff from going to work for your competitor!

★ **Treat your staff as "family."** I particularly like the idea of buying staff members lunch or dinner for their birthdays. This not only makes them feel special; more importantly, it allows them to see the restaurant from the other side of the table and to appreciate what the customer is thinking and feeling—and that is great training for their jobs. You may find that they come back from the experience with some suggestions for better service. That's the best result of all.

For the same reason, I like the concept of giving a staff discount to those who want to bring friends to the restaurant. This not only accomplishes the goals we mentioned above but also allows your staff to do what they should do best: serve as word-of-mouth advertisers for your restaurant. You may think that these groups are tying up tables that you would normally fill with "real" customers, but this is not so. They are enjoying themselves at your restaurant, building esprit de corps, receiving great training, and attracting new business in the form of their friends.

In the end, the best teams always win. Your job is to make sure that you are doing everything you can to give your team the training, support, and confidence that they need to win. Remember, when they win, you win.

DON'T FORGET TO FEED THE HORSES.

Staff retention is the single most significant challenge in our business. Training and education are certainly key ways to retain and to develop top-quality staff, but they are not the only things you can do, nor are they all you should do.

When you stop and think about it, you can control how you deal and interact with your employees, and employer-employee interaction is also an arena where you can have a meaningful impact on your restaurant.

Doing Like the Duke

A friend of mine used to start every day by visiting with each employee just for a minute or two. The conversation was simple: "How are you? How's your daughter? I like your new haircut. How do you like your new car?" When I asked him about his morning routine, his response surprised me.

"Remember those old John Wayne movies?" he asked. "When they rode into town, the first thing that the good guys did was feed and water the horses. Then they thought about themselves. My employees are my horses—without them, this place doesn't work. So the first thing I always do is feed and water the horses."

This great image has stayed with me through many jobs and many employees, and I follow my friend's lead. While I work hard at staff training and make sure that my staff is paid fairly, I also take the time, on a regular basis, to talk to my staff personally. I like to admire pictures of their children or hear about their family gatherings and weddings.

Listening to your employees is the most basic kind of employee management, and it is very important. How important? While making money is a major employee incentive (and, duh, doing your job better usually has a direct relationship to an increase in your earnings), job satisfaction is critical. Historically, employee studies have delineated two key points: first, that an occasional "atta boy" or "atta girl" (rewarding positive behavior) is monu-

A simple, look-you-in-the-eye thank you is a very powerful tool.

mentally important, and, second, that liking where you work and who you work with is as important as, if not more so than, the money.

Stoking Your Staff

Your customers always feel more comfortable seeing familiar faces, and they often develop relationships with your staff that are stronger than those with management. What does it take to keep those employees happy?

A simple, look-you-in-the-eye thank you is a very powerful tool. When do I say thanks? Every day.

I thank the employee who helped out when we needed it. I thank the employee who took a minute to look for the lost purse. I thank the employee who put in a double shift and looks as if he or she feels unappreciated.

I thank them because I know it makes a difference and because they have made a difference. For example, after a long night with a large party in the back room, sometimes the staff is exhausted. They should be, because they had a hard job. When they are ready to leave, I shake their hands and tell them that I appreciate their efforts, because I do appreciate their hard work and it would be stupid of me not to tell them. For those who left before I could make contact, I leave a sincere, handwritten Post-it on their time cards.

As a way of competing in this tough marketplace, I try to go beyond my competition to make my employees feel connected and appreciated. I send a card or flowers on special occasions. I have always believed in offering a free meal for two to any employee on his or her birthday, and I always make sure that there is a nice bottle of wine and a special dessert for them.

When you add up all this personal attention, it costs some money. But it is absolutely the best way I know to retain my employees and to keep them happy.

MONEY MAKES THE WORLD GO ROUND.

We have talked about staff retention from a number of different perspectives, and in the end, they all add up to one simple truth: The best way to retain your staff is to keep your staff happy. But while you can provide professional training and all the nice perks that a restaurant has to offer, the bottom line is always the same: Your workers will leave you if they are (or feel that they are) underpaid.

No matter how much time and energy you've invested in training and in keeping the staff focused and happy, you must remember what it's working for—money.

Pros' Payback

According to recent business surveys, it can cost $100,000 to replace a corporate employee—and that's money spent not on salary but on finding and training a qualified replacement. We sure don't spend that kind of money in our business, do we?

Well, maybe we do. All too often, we too complacently accept the fact that an employee is leaving, search the stack of recent applications for a likely suspect, and begin the process all over again: the training and the investment of energy and time. At some point you have to stop and ask yourself, isn't there a better way to do this?

I'm glad you asked, because I strongly believe that the true costs of losing a top service employee are higher than the basic expense of keeping one. Much higher. A good server will make sure that his or her guests enjoy themselves, and you can read the result on your bottom line; the average check is larger by as much as 30 percent when the real pros are working, because more appetizers, wine, and desserts are ordered.

Let's look at a top server's bottom-line impact in another way. If a good server handles 100 meals a night and can increase each tab by an average of $5, that's an extra $500 a night in your till. Multiply that by 20 days, and that

The true costs of losing a top service employee are higher than the basic expense of keeping one.

one server has increased revenue by $10,000 a month. How important is that business to you?

This doesn't even take into account the likelihood that those very happy customers will come back time and again or that they will tell their friends and associates, who may also come to dine in your restaurant.

Star Rewards

Repeat business and word-of-mouth publicity are the lifeblood of your business. You have to protect your star players from taking their skills—and perhaps your customers—to another restaurant. That means you have to compensate them enough to make them happy or run the risk of your establishment's becoming the restaurant world's equivalent of the Yankees, with all of your stars playing as "free agents."

All too often, restaurants assume that tips alone will provide the incentive for their service staff. I don't think that's the only answer.

I like to use financial incentive programs to build new parts of the business or a commission system that rewards employees who make a difference. I'm a believer in profit-sharing plans for key employees and even equity programs for key management personnel, and I strongly support paying those top service stars the salaries they deserve, which may include periodic cash bonuses. My position isn't based on nicety or a soft heart; it's a pragmatic business decision to make a restaurant as successful as it can be.

In the restaurant business, just like everywhere else, the best team usually wins. The restaurant manager or owner who knows how to build the best team has a huge advantage. That advantage pays off, year after year, when that same owner can keep his team working together, playing together and winning. In business, what you want is not just a winning season, but a long string of victories.

Keep your team together. Pay the pros what they deserve or watch the play-offs from the stands.

★ LET THE GAMES BEGIN!

Incentive programs can be a very effective way to boost your bottom line. A friendly staff competition of who can sell the most Chardonnay by the glass or the most slices of apple tart can be almost as fun as the reward. And a well-conceived contest gives employees a heightened focus on the tasks at hand—a highly desirable business objective. Even better, creating an incentive program requires very little financial investment.

Game Plan

All you need to raise employee morale and get that cash register ringing is to follow these few basic steps.

- ★ **Define your objective as specifically as possible and create concrete guidelines.** Whether the contest will entail selling the most appetizers, wines, or desserts per shift or garnering the most positive comment cards, every staff member should understand the objective and rules.
- ★ **Identify participating employees.** Does the program apply to full-time employees only, or can part-time people play? Do your best to be inclusive so that everyone can participate and build the sales momentum. I like to set up teams to promote camaraderie.
- ★ **Determine the duration of the contest and how you will measure results.** If there is too much time between the inception and reward, the excitement is lost. Four weeks is a good span, but don't overlook the boost you can encourage from a single-day or even a single-shift incentive.
- ★ **Set up a system that measures accomplishments daily, and post results weekly.** Everyone should understand the rules before the incentive program begins, and results should be displayed where everyone can track them.
- ★ **Decide how to pick and reward the winners.** You can create qualifications based on dollars, evaluations, or number of items sold. When you

choose the prize, make sure that it is appropriate and consider something other than money.

One way to increase the value of the reward is to trade with other restaurants or vendors and offer a dinner for two, gift certificate, or product. For example, if you reward winners with a nice watch, every time they look at it they will be reminded of their accomplishment. This is unlikely to happen if their cash prize pays an electric bill and is quickly forgotten.

Set the reward high enough to heighten the interest but not break the bank. A good prize standard is 5 to 10 percent of gross sales.

★ **Promote the incentive program with fanfare, and create an eye-catching display of the results.** Announce the contest during an employee meeting. Post a scorecard in an employee area or, if bingo is more your bag, create cards that encourage your team to accomplish all the tasks noted within each square. As you add marks of accomplishments, everyone can keep track of the stats. More importantly, a bold presentation will keep everyone interested in the game.

And the Winner Is . . .

When the winners of your contests are picked, make sure to celebrate the victories publicly. Post their photos on the bulletin board, give them a pat on the back at your staff meeting, and don't forget to say some kind words to those who did not win this go-around.

Once your incentive program is complete, go back to the drawing board and create a new competition with a different slant. If you find a way to ensure that the same people do not win every time, you will increase motivation among more of your staff.

When executed properly, incentive programs have no losers. Higher sales lead to larger tips, which will certainly boost morale, and staff appreciation and recognition add to employee confidence and happiness. And for any who have never tried, you'll be amazed at what you can accomplish. In the words of the great Woody Allen, 80 percent of success is just showing up. Trust me on this one . . . show up!

★ HOW DO YOU FIRE UP YOUR STAFF FOR SUCCESS?

In the previous essay I wrote about incentive programs—how contests, prizes, and public recognition, which are all forms of external motivation, help increase the bottom line and boost employee morale. This essay will examine types of internal motivation, which take less time and resources to implement and promise something even more valuable than money or gifts: heightened job satisfaction and employee loyalty.

Internal motivations have to do more with praise than prizes and gifts. When employees are acknowledged for their accomplishments, their self-esteem is raised, and as a consequence, they become happier and more productive. Programs to promote internal motivation are simple to execute. You need only show appreciation of each of your employees when you see them do something good and create a way to recognize this positive behavior.

Ways of Praise

There are a myriad of ways to recognize employees, build their internal motivation to exceed, and raise their level of job satisfaction. One method is what I call "atta boys," (and, of course, "atta girls") or verbal strokes, which can be given privately, semiprivately, or publicly. A private verbal stroke is as simple as pulling an employee aside and acknowledging him or her for a particular action or continued successes. This can be done on the spot, and immediate acknowledgement reinforces correct behaviors. Semipublic recognition could be a note on an employee's timecard or on the bulletin board. An example of public recognition is a verbal pat on the back during a staff meeting or daily lineup.

Verbal strokes may be nearly effortless, but I cannot overstate their power. Study after study has clearly shown that job satisfaction is at least as important as money in the workplace. Spreading the good word with accolades is one way to guarantee a higher level of happiness, whether it's in the kitchen, the office, or the dining room.

An "Employee of the Month" program is a more structured means to promote internal inspiration. Typically, such a program recognizes a staff member with a plaque or space of honor on the bulletin board. Some restaurants honor their employees behind the scenes, while others post information about their recognized employee in public spaces. In either case, all you need to do is set award criteria, create a space that honors winners, and go!

Promotion and Perks

Job promotion is among the strongest means to keep staff motivated. If employees believe that there is a real opportunity for advancement, they are less likely to become complacent. Any time there is an opening for a new position, promote from within, if possible. Move the dishwasher up to a busser or prep cook, bump up a busser to a server, or give an especially capable host a management position. You'll end up with proven employees in the strongest roles.

Classes and field trips are excellent methods for motivating your entire staff at once. Sessions in CPR or TOEFL (Teaching of English as a First Language) show employees that you are willing to invest to expand their knowledge and skills. Outings build esprit de corps and bring the kitchen and front-of-the-house staff together in a relaxed, nonwork setting. You don't have to take staff on Outward Bound–type experiences and have them jump off mountains! Take them to wineries or other restaurants, on picnics, or to do charity work. Outings help develop strong employee bonds, which also contribute to internal motivation.

Finally, let employees know that you are paying attention. Honor their birthdays by giving them a card or buying them dinner. Award job milestones with a free meal for two, a bonus, or, in extreme cases, equity.

The secret to nurturing internal motivations is to reward good behavior tangibly, proactively, regularly, and equally. Practice praising your staff on an ongoing basis, and you'll soon discover that your team is happier and more productive.

Spreading the good word with accolades is one way to guarantee a higher level of happiness, whether it's in the kitchen, the office, or the dining room.

★ THERE ARE NO SERVERS IN L.A.

There are only actors, screenwriters, and directors—all between jobs in Hollywood. It's an old joke, but all too often it rings true. Why do so many servers pass on a career in our industry?

Entry-level positions in restaurant service are attractive jobs to potential employees. Restaurants should be inundated with applicants, and in most cases, they are. So why is the turnover rate so high among servers?

Part of the answer to high turnover is that restaurant service is darned hard work, both physically and psychologically. The servers' stress levels can be high and the workload heavy. We have to expect a certain amount of washout. But there is an equally important reason why we lose so many of our staff each year: We don't give them enough reasons to stay.

Creating Career Paths

I've talked about offering appropriate compensation and creating a more pleasant work environment as a means of retaining staff. But if your employees don't understand why they might want to be working at your restaurant ten or twenty years from now, you will likely lose them. The lack of a clear career path for service professionals is an important issue for our entire industry.

We all know the standard progression—from busboy to server, from fast-food joint to fine-dining restaurant—but we must create further career paths for our service professionals, routes that involve higher pay, more recognition, and experiences and qualifications that will improve both their résumés and their futures.

Certainly, a service position at a top restaurant is a worthy career goal. But there ought to be more advanced positions that we encourage our top service staff to seek. Here are some of them:

★ **Sommelier.** If your wine sales are vitally important to your bottom line, a trained professional sommelier can increase these sales, provide more

> **If your employees don't understand why they might want to be working at your restaurant ten or twenty years from now, you will likely lose them.**

professional wine service, and attract a clientele that is interested in fine wine and willing to pay for it. This position comes with tangible and intangible rewards: income, prestige, and satisfaction.

★ **Wine Buyer.** Putting together a good wine list involves understanding a restaurant's mission statement, a clientele's preferences, and the intricate subtleties of wine. Promoting one of your top servers to this position gives him or her recognition and prestige that are rewarding on many levels.

★ **Staff Training Director.** If you have a server whose professionalism stands out above the rest, why not ask that server to direct your staff training? This will free up some of your time and also give that server a sense that his or her expertise is recognized and rewarded. Offering opportunities for personal growth helps to build careers.

★ **Manager.** This job is the ultimate opportunity for a super staffer. If you have hired wisely, you should have someone on your staff who might someday take over this position.

Spreading the Word

Good career opportunities exist at every restaurant, and this message must be communicated to the staff. They should know the qualifications and the additional education and experience needed for each job. And they should get that information the first day they are hired.

Communication is a critical factor in motivating employees to pursue industry careers. The Court of Master Sommeliers, the Master of Wine program, various schools of hospitality and hotel management, and local community colleges all offer courses that lead to the expertise and professionalism we want. But we have to make sure that the staff knows that these career-building programs exist. Once we have qualified personnel, we must promote them if we want to keep the top people on the staff and in the industry.

Retaining your best performers is always the key to great service.

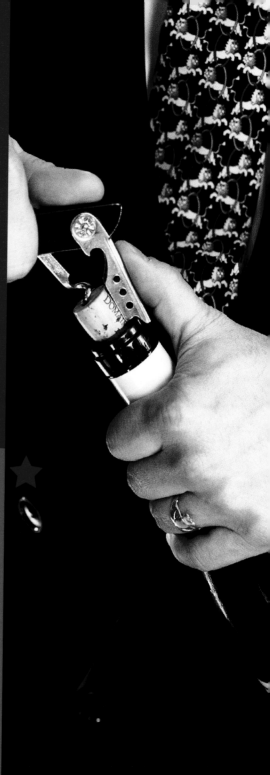

WINE SERVICE
★ ★ ★ ★

MOST RESTAURANTS TRAIN THEIR STAFF— THEY JUST DON'T DO ENOUGH.

In this terrible new world of continuing threats, we are all encouraged to get back to basics—family, friends, and the things that really matter. In our business, it is people who really matter.

I have often written about the ongoing and critical need for staff training. Why? Because training is the most important tool you have to improve your service staff's skills, and your service staff is the most vital nonfood or -kitchen asset of your restaurant. They truly are the people who matter for the continued well-being of your enterprise.

But I am continually surprised at the opportunities lost because of insufficient training. How does your staff education program measure up? In the following essays, we will examine what I believe every professional server should know about wine service, starting with the first training steps.

The Basics

Everyone on your staff who sells wine should know how to taste wine. You know the routine: look, swirl, smell, sip, savor, and swallow—or spit, if you are tasting more than a few wines! Your staff also should know how to look at the wine and why, what swirling accomplishes, what the bouquet tells us about a wine, why we swish the wine around in our mouths, and how the flavors and structure of the wine can affect the food it accompanies. This training is not a 15-minute "line-up" tasting before lunch or dinner; it's a dedicated couple of hours of instruction, complete with real-life applications and tastings.

Everyone who serves wine in a restaurant should have a good understanding of the wine-service process or ritual. This should include everything from how to open, present, and pour a bottle of wine to which wineglasses are appropriate, which guests should be served first, and how to refill the glasses as the diners proceed with their meal. Of course, role-playing different scenarios is a very beneficial training technique.

In addition to the service itself, your staff should understand how to sell wine in a restaurant setting. They should know how to explain wines to customers who have not tasted them and how to suggest wines to customers who are looking for educated advice. They should be able to distinguish between a wine expert and a novice and to adjust their advice accordingly.

This last element of service knowledge is something that cannot be taught in a single sitting; we all learn more about "reading" our customers every day as we work at our jobs. As we gain experience, we begin to recognize customers who want something a little special or who are looking to impress a business associate, and we learn to distinguish between them and the customers who are on a first date and may be watching their budget closely. Each customer is a new opportunity and a new experience. Nevertheless, the basics can be covered and the important issues raised in an hour of discussion and role-playing.

Finally, your service staff should know which wines pair best with which meals on the menu. And they should know why. As you add dishes, change wines, or refine recipes, you will need to update this education so that your servers don't fall behind. Good training is a never-ending process.

Taking Advantage

If you have been keeping score all along, covering the basics adds up to at least five hours of staff training. That's a lot of time and energy—and money, since you'll have to pay your staff to come in to attend these sessions. But it is also the best investment you can make. It will help your staff take advantage of the opportunities that arrive during every interaction with your customers—opportunities to build closer relationships, introduce a customer to a new experience or sensation, sell wine, and meet and exceed expectations.

Those are opportunities that you cannot afford to let pass.

In addition to the service itself, your staff should understand how to sell wine in a restaurant setting.

★ WINE TRAINING DOESN'T END WITH THE BASICS.

In our business, there is nothing more basic than the need for staff training. Staff education not only improves your restaurant, but it also sends two important messages to your staff: first, you believe in service as a profession and are doing what you can to help them succeed in their chosen career; and second, you care about them and want to help them to be successful. After all, if they are successful in your restaurant, you will be the first to know!

Four wine-related elements of training are absolutely essential for any restaurant service professional: how to taste wine, the service ritual, how to sell wine, and wine-and-food matching. But once your staff learns the fundamentals, it would be wrong to consider your job done. For those diners who really love wine—and buy it—you need to offer something more. Send your service staff out to the front lines armed with information.

Beyond the Basics

Your senior service staff and those who interact the most with your guests should know how red, white, and rosé wines are made, that it involves more than just adding yeast to crushed grapes and sitting back to enjoy the show. They should know the subtleties of how temperature affects fermentation, how oak affects the flavor of a wine, what residual sugar is, and why some wineries use malolactic fermentation.

Your staff should know what effect these techniques have on the finished flavors of wine. Why? Because many of your customers will know at least some of this, and you want your staff to be able to meet them halfway. Yes, this means more staff training—at least another hour of instruction with tastings to illustrate the various techniques mentioned above.

Of course, every winemaker will tell you that wines are made in the vineyard as much as they are in the winery. And because they have also told this to your wine-savvy customers, your staff should know how to grow grapes, too. No, they don't have to know the difference between bilateral cordon and partial Smart-Dyson trellising systems! But they do have to know what effect irrigation has on wine quality, why yields are so important to making good wine, what hillside slopes and exposures do to the quality of the grapes, and what are the basic University of California at Davis heat summation regions. Yep, another hour of training, along with a tasting or two.

They also should know about wine packaging—what a capsule is and why it is on the bottle, the various kinds of corks (and screw caps), and how they affect the wine. They should know how to read a label and understand the meaning of all of the various terms listed on it. In short, they should be able to explain every part of the wine bottle that they present to your customers. If they cannot, they are certain to miss opportunities. This last topic should take at least an hour to explore.

Outside Help

Hey, stop that! I can see you rolling your eyes from here! You don't have to do all this training yourself. You can take advantage of winemakers or distributor reps who stop in to make sure you are selling their wine. Ask them if they wouldn't mind leading a staff-training session that would explain one of the three topics I've mentioned. In most cases, they will agree.

The winemakers or reps will agree because they know that this time spent with your staff will help their business. Their expertise will help your staff to sell more wine—and more of their wine. And they will do it because they know that you run the kind of restaurant that takes the time to train the staff well and, in doing so, becomes successful.

Which is exactly why *you* should do it, too.

For those diners who really love wine—and buy it—you need to offer something more.

WHAT DO ALL THE BEST SERVERS IN THE WORLD HAVE IN COMMON?

Are they all men? Do they all speak French? Are they all very outgoing and friendly? Are they Master Sommeliers? Nope. But they do know the food and wine of the restaurant in which they work—inside and out. That's a real competitive advantage and one that your servers can't learn on their own.

If you want your staff to be able to provide sound, helpful advice to your customers, you must give them the tools and the training they need to do it right. By "training," I mean more than just letting them taste the dishes on the menu with a few random glasses of wine. Food-and-wine pairing is a discipline that is both a science and an art, and you will need to give your staff a basic education in its fundamentals.

Pairings 101

In short, you will need to explain why we serve white wine with fish and red wine with beef—and, often, why we don't. Also, if you really want to do the job right, you should give your waitstaff practical experience—the chance to taste crab cakes with Cabernet Sauvignon and a heavily oaked Chardonnay with raw shellfish. It's a lot easier to understand (and sell) what works after you experience what doesn't work.

Start with a single, simple concept: The wine should match the sauce of the entrée. Let your staff taste calamari with a slice of lemon, and then ask them to match it with a wine. They will quickly find that the lemon captures much of what we want in our perfect wine match: fresh, lively, crisp, and refreshing sensations. That says Sauvignon Blanc or Muscadet to me. Then try the calamari with a tartarlike mayonnaise, a spicy pungent sauce that is perhaps on the sweeter side (something Thai or Vietnamese), and see if the same wines still go best. Let them discover that there are other wines that might match better, such as sparkling or even light reds.

Chicken with white wine? Not always. Coq au vin will match up much better with a soft red wine that works well with the flavors and character of the red-wine sauce; a Pinot Noir will usually be a better choice than a

> All great servers know how to listen. And when it comes to making customers happy, no other technique comes close.

Sauvignon Blanc. Spaghetti with a tomato-based sauce? I often do like something rich, red, and sassy—Chianti, for example. But put that same pasta in a cream sauce with garlic, and I will reach for a bottle of Pinot Grigio or Chardonnay.

It takes time, commitment, and energy to give your staff this kind of education. It's not enough for you to describe these pairings; they have to taste and experience them, as well. You don't have to work your way through the entire menu and wine list, but you should give your staff the basic information they need to approach food-and-wine pairing with confidence.

Breaking the Rules

All great servers know how to listen. And when it comes to making customers happy, no other technique comes close. If a customer wants to drink Riesling with his osso buco alla Milanese, your server should be comfortable with serving him the best darn Riesling on the list. Remember that restaurant guests run the gamut in taste preferences. A classic French culinary tradition works well for many diners, but others may prefer something completely different. Please don't make the mistake of enforcing the so-called rules of wine-and-food pairing on a customer who knows what he or she wants. I can't think of a better recipe for disaster.

To be successful, a server has to know the rules of wine-and-food pairing and then have the confidence to break them whenever it will make the customer happy. A server like that will keep your customers smiling, meal after meal.

SUPERIOR WINE SERVICE STARTS WITH MASTERING THE BASICS.

We've outlined some great tips for superior table service. It's now time to outline some techniques that can move your wine service up a notch.

Setting the Table

Let's start with the cover or place setting. I recommend pre-setting stemware along with the water glass for one big reason and a somewhat sneaky one: It suggests to the guest that wine is on the dining agenda, and it works as a subliminal sales tool. Of course, if guests decline wine, remove the glasses.

Placement of the initial wineglass is always on the right, above the main-course knife. When serving multiple wines, I like to add glasses from the left to the right, so that with each added wine "course," pouring over the previous glasses is avoided. If you are removing the used glass after each course, it makes sense to place the four or five glasses that you will be using in advance, and then begin filling them from the right. As you remove each glass, you will be removing the end glass. This method eliminates messy filling and removal and makes for a much simpler and cleaner presentation overall.

Proper Wine Temperatures

Now, let's talk about wine temperatures. I feel as if I've been saying this forever, but I still see wines being served at inappropriate temperatures, so I need to keep mentioning it!

White wines should be served chilled, but not glacially cold. Of course, sparkling and lighter white wines can take a serious chilling, but all nuances are lost in an overly icy California Chardonnay or white Burgundy. An ideal serving temperature range for white wines is 45° to 55°F.

Red wines are often served too warm. The room temperature that we all enjoy living in is not the perfect serving temperature for reds. Cellar temperature and serving temperature should be 55° to 65°F. For Beaujolais, Dolcetto, young Riojas, and some Pinot Noirs, a slight chill can optimize each wine's attributes. A quick trip to a bucket of ice and water can really pay off with these wines, especially if they are initially on the warm side. A general rule: fruity reds with low tannins benefit from chilling; higher-tannin, big wines should be less chilled, as chilling accentuates the tannins, and, ergo, the wine's bitter components.

Serving the Wine

Now that we have the table set and the wines at the right temperatures, let's talk about the actual service of the wine.

Repeat the wine information back to the guest before reaching for your corkscrew. It's better to find out that the vintage has been changed or the wine was misfiled before you open it, rather than afterward.

Where do you actually open the wine? The best setting is a wine cart or side table, but you don't see these very often in America. The next best option is on the table, placed on a wine coaster or bread and butter plate, to the right of the host, with the wine label facing the host. Check the wine's temperature at this point to see if it would benefit from chilling.

After you have opened the wine, the rule of thumb is to wipe with a napkin two times. Wipe the bottle neck and cork once after removing the capsule to get rid of any mold or other matter. Wipe the bottle rim again after removing the cork to eliminate any tartrates or sediment that might be present at the rim of the bottle. With all of the new wine closures on the market, these rules should still hold true. Even if there probably isn't mold or sediment, the whole process is what makes theater out of wine service.

Pre-setting stemware along with the water glass suggests to the guest that wine is on the dining agenda, and it works as a subliminal sales tool.

WHAT SEPARATES COMPETENT FROM FABULOUS WINE SERVICE? THEATER.

In the previous essay, we outlined ways to move your wine service abilities up a notch. From properly setting the table with stemware to finding the best place on the tabletop to gracefully open the bottle, good wine service takes some solid floor experience and problem-solving skills.

Sure, the mechanics need to be there, but there's that element of drama and flair that captivates even the most stoic wine fan. It's that extra flourish, the impeccable removal of a foil or polished decanting techniques, that make the procedure appear effortless. These are the types of skills that move your wine service onto a higher plane.

Study the Pros

The theater of wine service can take years to perfect, but having an awareness of it is a good start on the road to mastery. Educational programs, such as classes from the Court of Master Sommeliers, the Allied Domecq Academy of Wine and Service Excellence, the Sommelier Society of America, and others can be very helpful.

While understanding wine and service through taking classes can provide background, being mentored by someone whom you trust and respect is the best way to really "own" wine service. Perhaps you are fortunate enough to work with a real pro on a daily basis. Observation will help you pick up tricks and save yourself some trial and error, but practicing what you learn is what will really make the difference. As with anything else that you are learning, ask lots of questions and challenge the teacher. These are the best avenues for mastery.

Sure, the mechanics need to be there, but there's that element of drama and flair that captivates even the most stoic wine fan.

More Basic Tricks

Of course, we all need to hone our wine-service basics before we can really dig into the theatrical elements. Here are some valuable suggestions that will serve you well.

★ **When pouring a taste for the person who ordered the wine, pour an ounce or so.** It's very hard to taste wine when you have only three or four drops with which to work. Also, when two or more people are involved in choosing the wine, pour a taste for all concerned, and then stand back to receive feedback from both or all of them.

★ **Proper wine service at a table always goes in the clockwise direction.** Traditional service calls for serving women first, men second, and the host last, regardless of gender. If the party contains eight or more, serve in the clockwise direction, regardless of gender, ending with the host. Be prepared to bend the rules: For example, a table of business-men from Japan with their wives will expect the men to be served first.

★ **Upon completion of pouring and before actually removing the cork from the table, ask the host if you may take it away.** Someone may want to save it as a souvenir from a special occasion. I've seen more than a few servers who end up fishing through the trash bins because they did not ask; that's neither fun nor efficient.

★ **Large parties (eight or more) can be a real pouring challenge.** Often, only one bottle of each wine is being ordered, so gauge pours carefully to ensure that everyone receives one!

★ **If you observe that a guest is left-handed, discretely move his or her glass-ware to the left side.** The customer may not say anything but will appreciate your thoughtful gesture.

Master the List

Of course, thinking about wine service is difficult without considering the knowledge of wine that any excellent wine professional must possess. No matter how often it changes, make sure that you have working familiarity with your establishment's wine list and that you are especially conversant in all of the wines sold by the glass. Guests learning about wine for the first time often begin by ordering wine by the glass. Knowing how to discuss these wines in a user-friendly manner will all but guarantee future wine sales.

HOW TO RUIN A PERFECTLY GOOD BOTTLE OF WINE.

I know, I know. Our job is to make sure that everything goes well, from soup to nuts. Then why do so many restaurants make basic wine-service mistakes that drive away customers?

We all know that when customers order wine, we should display the bottle so that they can verify that we have provided the right producer, varietal, and vintage. But that's not nearly enough. When you stop to think of it, most of the bottles of wine on your list cost more than an entrée and have significant profit margins. Doesn't it make sense to spend the same type of time and attention on your wine service that you do with the food? Here are three absolutely necessary wine-service rules.

1. **Serve wines at their proper temperatures.** Your customers have every reason to expect that the wine they order will be served at the appropriate temperature. A great bottle of wine is a memorable experience for your guests, but you can easily destroy that delightful memory by serving the wine too warm or too cold.

    If you have to choose one or the other, too cold is better. With time, a cold wine will warm up in your dining room, but a wine that is too warm is simply not enjoyable. We all know that white wines should be served chilled, and every restaurant has a cold box and ice buckets for this purpose. Yet why are so many white wines served too warm?

    When a white wine is in the glass, it should be just cold enough for condensation to form on the outside of the glass; 50 to 55°F is about right. No condensation? Get a cooler bottle or go for an ice bucket, right away; don't wait for the customer to ask for one.

    Don't make the mistake of assuming that this is primarily a problem with white wines. In my experience, restaurants are more likely to serve red wines too warm. Why? The conventional wisdom is that red wines are to be served at room temperature, which is true if you live

Doesn't it make sense to spend the same type of time and attention on your wine service that you do with the food?

in a chateau in France or England, where this practice began. For the rest of us, the wine should be served at closer to 60°F. If your dining room is this cold, you have other problems!

Wines that are too warm seem heavier, more alcoholic, and lifeless. They do not refresh the palate and are not flattering to any cuisine. Why would any restaurant want its food and wines to clash rather than harmonize, especially when the solution is so obvious and so easy?

2. **Serve your wine in nice stemware.** No, you don't need to spend a fortune, but if you are selling wines on your list for more than $40 per bottle, you should have appropriate wineglasses. Open and larger bowls for red wines, thin rims, and elegant stems all make a wine taste much better. The glasses don't have to cost as much as the wine, but serving a $50 bottle of wine in clunky $2 glasses is an insult to the wine and to the customer. And don't forget: The customer who orders the best bottle of wine on your list is the one that you most want to keep happy!

3. **Glasses should be sparkling clean and free from odors.** Make sure that your dishwashing routine includes a good rinse cycle, so that the glasses don't smell like chlorine or soap. You wouldn't want your crème brûlée to taste like a swimming pool, and the same is true for your wines. If necessary, rinse the glasses again in plain water to eliminate any residual odors.

One more thing: I have also been served a perfect wine, at a perfect temperature, in a perfectly shaped glass, only to discover that the glass has come directly from the dishwasher and is still warm. The result? The wine is spoiled, and so is your reputation.

There is an old saying that God is in the details. You may not find religion by observing these rules, but you will find that your customers are happier, your wine and food tastes better, and your restaurant is more successful.

WHY DO WE HAVE WINE-SERVICE TRADITIONS?

Many owe their existence to the clouded past of history—when ships were of wood and the men of iron. Do they really have any relevance to today's world of teleconferencing and on-line ordering? Not surprisingly, some do and some don't.

Cork Customs

When you present a wine bottle to the host of the table, you are really just asking him or her to confirm that the wine you are serving is the one that was ordered. This pretty basic action has changed very little over time. Even in this rapidly changing world, it is nice to know that there are some traditions that remain constant.

On the other hand, some wine-service customs have radically changed. When you strip off the capsule from a wine bottle, you are removing what once was a rat-proofing device. The old lead-foil capsules would poison the rats in your cellar before the vermin could chew up the vastly more edible corks.

Today, many wineries have decided to go without the capsule completely, while others use clear plastic or even a top dot of sealing wax. The purpose, other than simply to look nice, is to provide a barrier to product tampering. That is not an altogether modern concept! (Stay tuned.)

The cork was originally presented to the diner to indicate that it was truly from the winery on the label. In the days of bottlings in various locations, the cork, far more than the label, was an accurate indicator of the bottle's provenance. Now that most fine wines are bottled at the château or winery, the issue of provenance is far less important. Many modern corks identify both the vintage and the producer. This custom originated so that the owner knew that the wine bottle hadn't been refilled with some Château Rotgut by a mischievous operator.

When you place the cork unobtrusively on the table near the host, you are merely allowing an inspection, if the host so desires. The gesture is not a sug-

As the official taster for the manor or castle, the sommelier was supposed to taste each wine to make sure that it would not poison anyone.

gestion to the host that he or she spend some time evaluating the quality of the cork, the number of growth rings in the bark, or the moisture content. If the wine tastes good, the cork matters little!

Pouring Practices

Pouring the host a small taste of wine is perhaps the oldest wine-service tradition. Today, this courtesy allows the host to make sure that the wine is sound and displays the wine's true character. This service nicety protects guests from a poorly selected or stored bottle.

The original custom, however, is quite the opposite! In the feudal age of lords and ladies, the host's vessel was poured first, so that he could assure his guests that he was not trying to poison them—at least not with wine. Poisoning was a popular political strategy in those days, and dinner invitations from the castle next door must have been received as a mixed blessing!

The tradition of the sommelier arose during medieval times. As the official taster for the manor or castle, the sommelier was supposed to taste each wine to make sure that it would not poison anyone. One hopes that he was paid more than minimum wage plus tips for that kind of work!

The specific pouring order depended on local custom. While some may have poured the guest of honor first, and others the royal family and then guests, we now have a straightforward and simple protocol: Start with the diner to the immediate right of the host, and pour around the table in a counterclockwise direction, finishing up with the host.

In an age when social status, position, and success were all reflected in one's position at the dinner table, service issues were of vital concern. In today's more egalitarian society, service rules have simply become a reasonable and efficient way for diners and the waitstaff to work together toward a great dining experience—which is to say, they still matter.

SERVICE PROFESSIONALS SEEM TO FALL ON ONE SIDE OF THE FOOD-AND-WINE "FENCE" OR THE OTHER.

They are either very strong on food with little wine knowledge or vice versa. The result of these "imbalances" is that food-and-wine pairing is much more of a challenge than it should be. Having a more balanced understanding of food and wine and the way that they interact will bring your service to an even higher level.

First of all, let's think about keys. They get you in and out of the house, your car out of the garage, and important papers into your safe-deposit box. When considering matching wine and food, understanding the keys of what make a food and a wine compatible are also critically essential. Not all wines are created equal, and because a Cabernet Sauvignon is not a Pinot Noir and a Chardonnay is not a Chenin Blanc, it is not possible to make blanket statements about wines and their food affinity. Many people like to keep things easy, and the color-coding that dominates most Americans' theories on why food and wine work (red wine with meat and white wine with fish) are only partially correct.

There are five keys to wine—building blocks of a wine's personality that make it more or less food friendly. Let's take a look at them.

Acidity

Without question, if I had only one wine trait to work with to reach culinary happiness, it would be the wine's acidity level—its tartness factor. All wines have acid, but not all have it to an equal degree. For wine to be food affectionate, it must have ample acidity. We are not talking electricity here, but the wine should have a nice bite. Acidity acts with food in several ways. First, it provides cut or contrast to richness and fat. Most cream- or butter-based sauces or the oiliness associated with your favorite pizza require the refreshing foil of high acidity to provide a crisp contrast. In addition, acidity imitates lemon, and any time you find that a wedge of lemon would make something better, such as a simple sautéed breast of chicken, a broiled piece of fish, or a side of steamed vegetables, a wine's acidity will mimic the lemon to help

There are five keys to wine—building blocks of a wine's personality that make it more or less food friendly.

bring out the flavor of the dish. Finally, for foods with some tartness, such as vinaigrettes, acid in wine is the only way to prevent feeling as if you are drinking a glass of sharp, nondescript water with a bad attitude.

Sweetness

Actual sweetness in wine takes on two forms. The first is the obvious high level of sugar associated with a dessert wine or sweet, fortified wine, such as Port. Here it is mandatory that the level of sweetness in the wine is at least on a par with that in the dessert, or your wine will taste quite unpleasant. (Remember sweet wedding cake with that flute of sparkling wine?) The sweet sugar of dessert wines, however, can have fun with salt. The time-honored combinations of blue-veined cheese with Sauternes or late-harvest Sauvignon Blanc and England's classic Port with Stilton are based on this phenomenon. An enjoyable third-party flavor is formed in your mouth when these taste worlds collide.

The second form of sugar is the semisweet level found in Chenin Blanc or Riesling. A balance of sweet and sour can be marvelous with a variety of dishes. Slight sweetness can offset aromatic levels of spice. A touch of capsicum will seem toned down when accompanied by an off-dry white, and while there are virtually no wines that go with the spiciest dish at your preferred Thai restaurant, moderate levels of heat are simple to work around. Also, a little bit of sweetness can mirror a similar quality in the food with which it is paired. A bright, off-dry Vouvray as a tablemate to venison with dried cherries will exhibit this quite nicely.

Alcohol

Wine without alcohol is difficult to imagine—it's so fundamental. Yet the larger the dose of it, the less flexible you will find the wine to be. Wines of

Tannin is most happy with fat and protein; hence the obvious affinity of massive reds with red meat and full-flavored cheese.

moderate alcohol are almost always better food matches than those more generously endowed. Alcohol is exaggerated by food, and depending on what you are eating, this may not be desirable. If you are having a delicate dish with a "big" wine, the alcohol of that wine will squash the subtlety of the food.

In addition, this exacerbated alcohol phenomenon can be extremely unpleasant with spicy food; your mouth will feel as if you've literally dumped alcohol onto the fire and made things worse. Big wines require big food, so when you pull out that bottle of full-throttle Zinfandel, opt for a thick juicy burger, rather than a gently grilled poussin!

Oak

What would Chardonnay be without oak? How could you otherwise enhance the complexity of a Cabernet Sauvignon blend? Unoaked Chardonnay and Cabernet seem almost implausible, and many of us would not enjoy our wines were it not for the nuances imparted on them by the gradual aging of those wines in oak barrels.

You should be aware, however, that while those flavors may seem appropriate in the context of the solo wine performance, they may strike discordant notes when that same wine is matched up with your favorite entrée. Oak, in my opinion, becomes a segregated element when accompanying food, and if you have ever found yourself describing a wine as being "too oakey," you'll really be sent reeling. Oakey wines with meals very often can create the experience of wine, food, and a lumberyard. Now, if you are completely enamored with the flavors of barrels, this is a plus. But if you find oak occasionally overwhelming, trust me, you'll feel as if you've been sucking on toothpicks. Wines with lower or moderate oak influences or even wines sans oak are generally better table companions.

Tannin

Red wines have tannin. It allows those wines to age and is a significant part of their personality. While a Pinot Noir may possess much less than a Syrah, it has some. Tannin, whether imparted to the wine through barrel aging, skin contact, or a combination of both, is very much like alcohol. The more there is, the more limited you are when matching with food.

Tannin is an astringent that seeks something to latch on to when it enters your mouth. It is most happy with fat and protein; hence the obvious affinity of massive reds with red meat and full-flavored cheese. In the absence of these food components, however, tannin will grab on to anything it can, such as your tongue, your gums, or the roof of your mouth, leaving you with that Al Jolson pucker.

If you plan on serving a rich, youthful red wine, take a lesson from those folks in Bordeaux who generally serve the same meal to visitors lucky enough to dine at their châteaux: Choose a slab of steak and simple vegetables and/or potatoes. The Bordelais know that the wine requires the meat to smooth out those tannins and to allow the succulent fruit to glow. When you want to enjoy lighter meals or foods that are not exclusively the domain of carnivores, select red wines with light, transparent tannins: Pinot Noir, Gamay, or Dolcetto nicely fit the bill.

Well, there you have them. The five keys to wine. Use these keys well, and you'll find that all the gastronomic doors will open with minimal, if any, struggle.

Alcohol is exaggerated by food, and depending on what you are eating, this may not be desirable.

SPECIALTY SERVICE
★★★★★

DINING ALONE? HOW ABOUT THE TABLE BY THE LADIES' ROOM?

The single diner presents a unique set of challenges for the waitstaff. Please don't look at solitary diners as odd pieces of a jigsaw puzzle, to be fit in wherever and whenever you can make a spot for them. While they certainly don't represent the profitability of a group of eight on an expense-account dinner, solitary diners are customers, and they deserve the same respect and service as any other party in the restaurant.

Seating Arrangements

Almost everything in a restaurant, from the size of the tables to the size of a typical bottle of wine, is designed for at least two. I frequently see solitary diners being directed toward the bar for their dinners, leaving tables available in the restaurant for larger groups. If customers are willing, this may be a workable solution, but they should never be made to feel that they are unwelcome in the main restaurant. After all, if you please your solo patrons, they may come back in three weeks with business colleagues, family, or a group of friends.

Today, some restaurants have revived an old tradition by offering a large "community" table, where individuals or couples can drop in and join other diners. The restaurant manages to use only one table for these small groups, and sometimes diners welcome the chance for some impromptu conversation with new acquaintances. This practical tactic works only if the diners are going to be comfortable with a communal seating arrangement. Single diners should never be forced to sit at such a table.

Menu Flexibility

Portion size can be a concern for the solo diner. While larger groups often will order a selection of appetizers (or even entrées) to be shared among the group, the lone diner has fewer readily available options. As the larger group joyously tastes through your menu, the single diner is left to choose only one among your many specialties.

Take the time to give your
best service to every diner in your
restaurant, whether they be the
magnanimous host of a party of twelve or
a solo diner reading *War and Peace.*

If possible, try to offer a sampler menu of some of your more popular appetizers as a separate item on the menu. The solitary diner will be delighted with the opportunity to taste the best of what your kitchen has to offer, and you may be surprised to see that small groups may choose to order this menu choice with wild abandon. If you're not too busy in the kitchen, allow the servers a little leeway and creativity in mixing and matching. Menu flexibility may lead to a big payoff! Degustation menus are often embraced by the single diner as a way to experiment.

Customized Service

Your by-the-glass program always should be designed so that your waitstaff knows exactly which selections are the best matches with each of the dishes on your menu. This approach to service is a big help to the solitary diner. It also benefits a member of a large group who orders a very different set of menu selections and prefers a by-the-glass choice, rather than a share of the bottle ordered by the rest of the group.

Finally, a brief note about table-service manners for the lone diner. Take the time to listen; with good interpersonal skills, you will quickly determine whether your diner wants to be left alone to his or her thoughts or whether he or she would appreciate a little conversation to break up the meal. In most cases, solitary diners will respond well to a slightly increased amount of conversation with the waitstaff.

Take the time to give your best service to every diner in your restaurant, whether they be the magnanimous host of a party of twelve or a solo diner reading *War and Peace.* Remember, the best single source of new business for your restaurant is sitting at your tables every night. You never want to give your customers a reason to go somewhere else the next time!

★ DINING AND FAMILIES: LIFE BEYOND THE HAPPY MEAL.

Families dining today are looking for more than a home-cooked meal. Their number one reason for dining out is to spend quality time together, away from the distractions of home life.

With the increase in dual-income families and the growth in the numbers of people working at home, it's no wonder that people need to leave their homes to interact with their families. Most families dine out an average of five times per month for dinner and twice a month for lunch. This is good news for restaurants that understand these diners and how to satisfy their needs.

What are diners with children looking for in a restaurant? Friendly service is number one, followed by value and family atmosphere. Rude table service and slow service were cited as the most annoying dining problems.

Customers with children can be a nightmare or your ticket to success, depending upon how you and your staff manage them. A restaurant cannot sacrifice its customer base to please kids, nor can it compromise its concept, because it will risk alienating both its core customers and its staff. Rather than using special pricing and expensive gimmicks, such as a $1.99 kid menu or a parading clown, you and your staff must concentrate on the personal level—service.

I've developed these basic guidelines and suggestions:

★ **Hungry kids are cranky kids.** By the time a family decides to go out to dinner, picks a restaurant, and actually walks in the door, 45 to 60 minutes may have passed. The kids will be ravenous and cross. Make sure that bread and water are on the table immediately upon seating. If they order drinks, make sure that the drinks are delivered immediately as well. (A drink cover is a good idea for your young guests!) The good news here is that tables with kids turn more quickly than others, so keeping families moving will increase your business and make them happy, too!

★ **Bored kids are crabby kids.** If your establishment has coloring materials, games, or other kid giveaways, use them. If you don't have these things, consider creating some. A few crayons and some photocopies of pictures to color can go a long way.

★ **Entertained kids are happy, and so are their parents.** The number one service trick for handling families is to play to the kids immediately. Use a squeaky clean joke, a funny face, small talk about something that they're wearing, or anything else that works for you to win over the kids. Their parents will notice that their load has been lightened and will come back for that reason. Keeping the tables of families happy is important to their satisfaction but also to the overall enjoyment of the other diners on your floor. Who doesn't need another great way to build repeat business?

★ **Never underestimate the value of a maraschino cherry!** Gimmicks work, whether it's a cherry in their drink, a special ceremony around entrées or desserts, or a children's menu full of foods that kids like. Experiment with your own ideas to see what works and what doesn't.

I can't emphasize strongly enough just how important families can be to your business base. If children are clamoring to go to your establishment because they always have a great time, their parents are more likely to dine there. I find that many establishments are overlooking this loyal and profitable business segment. View your treatment of kids as business development!

What are diners with children looking for in a restaurant? Friendly service is number one, followed by value and family atmosphere.

DON'T OVERLOOK THE DOMESTIC TOURIST.

There are unique challenges to working with homegrown tourists, and if you perform well, your business will prosper even while your local clientele leaves town for their vacations.

Who are they? Families on vacation are often easy to spot: Their shorts, Hawaiian shirts, and cameras strung about their necks are dead giveaways. A strong regional accent from a different part of the country is another clue. Others may be part of a conference or on a business trip, adding a few days on the end of the visit for some sightseeing and R&R.

Identifying these customers and meeting their wishes matters to your business. They are likely to have a special set of interests and needs. They may be slightly tired from their travels and a little bit lost and dazed. If your restaurant can develop a reputation for treating them with TLC, you can make a real difference in their visit and also in your restaurant's bottom line, via the positive word of mouth that they'll share when they return home.

Turning Tables and Charming Children

If your customers come from the opposite coast, chances are that they are on a slightly different time schedule. While your regulars may fight over the 8:00 reservation slots, you might find that your tourist guests want to eat early or late. This is an enormous opportunity for you to make a new set of customers happy.

Make sure that your staff greets those 5:30 reservations with the same enthusiasm that they would a favorite regular customer at 8:00. You not only will make their experience more memorable, but also you will turn an extra table that night—and as we all know, fuller early seatings are among the easiest ways to increase profits.

Adults may be a bit out of sorts from jet lag, but when you upset the schedule of children, you change their lives; if the kids are cranky, nobody has a good time. If your staff can be sensitive to children's needs, their parents will be indebted to you for far more than just a meal! Make sure that

> Satisfied tourists not only will tell their friends at home about your restaurant, but they also will tell their fellow guests *and* the concierge at the hotel.

you serve children something to eat or drink quickly and provide special personal attention up front. A new face to talk to is real entertainment for a child on the road.

While your regulars may stick to menu favorites, tourists often are seeking a memorable wine-and-food experience. They may be more likely to experiment with the menu, test the kitchen, and explore your wine list. If you make them happy, you will reap the rewards. Satisfied tourists not only will tell their friends at home about your restaurant, but they also will tell their fellow guests *and* the concierge at the hotel. When that happens, you can expect to see a lot more guests from that hotel every night, and that will make you more than just a good restaurant—it will make you a destination!

An Extra Service

Finally, tourists may need more than food and drink. They are lonely, far from home, and a little unsure of their surroundings. Our best vacations involve getting to know someone in the area, having a guide who lets us in on the local secrets and makes us feel welcome and valued.

Some might argue that this is the job of a hotel concierge, not the restaurant. I believe a good restaurant can and should provide some of these same services to its customers, both because they want the service and because it is simply good business. If your staff can supply the inside scoop on how to enjoy your city, the new customers will remember that far more than the food or wine. You will have made that most important connection—the one between people.

Work with your staff to make sure that they understand the needs of these visitors and how you can all help make their visit memorable, for them and for you!

DIVERSITY IS A HOT TOPIC THESE DAYS.

How many of us consider carrying diversity awareness out onto the floor? The "never judge a book by its cover" rule is fully applicable in the dining room, where it can have a real financial impact. Potentially lucrative opportunities abound in your dining room, and they come in all shapes and sizes.

Marketing to Women. If wine education is used as a measure, then wine knowledge is increasing among women faster than men. For example, at Pat Fegan's Chicago Wine School, 80 percent of the students are female. Also, I've noticed that more women are taking charge in restaurants, especially female executives who are entertaining business clients. To serve women better, here are some suggestions:

★ Don't automatically hand the wine list to a man if a woman appears to be the host. You can introduce it and watch for cues from the table for the handoff, or you can gracefully leave it in a central location after bringing it to the attention of the table.

★ In social situations, don't cater to the men at the table at the expense of the women in the party. Again, watch for cues from the table. Pour tastes of the wine for more than one person in the party if they seem to be making collective wine decisions.

One of my biggest pet peeves is the moaning that I hear from servers when they see a table of women sit down in their sections. In many restaurants, women are branded with a reputation for ordering appetizers or salads, having one nonalcoholic beverage, and leaving light tips. This negative generalization should be resisted by your waitstaff. A group of women might be event planners that could bring profitable future business to your establishment, or they could be bank presidents, college professors, or college students. You really can't tell, so don't assume anything!

It is much easier to retain a customer than to bring in a new one.

More and more, *women* are the ones making the dining decisions. So if they order only a salad and iced tea by day, their comfort and sense of service will influence whether they will return with their mates for a more elaborate meal.

The Single Diner. Another customer who remains undervalued is the single diner, female or male. In many restaurants, I think we tend to view "single-ness" with a sense of pathos, but in most cases, nothing could be further from the truth. Often, a single guest is traveling on business or trying to complete work over dinner. He or she may not be having the same convivial experience as the rest of the room and may not want it. Here are some suggestions to serve single diners better:

* ★ For hosts, a general goal should be to respect a person's choice to dine alone and then to make the experience at your restaurant as positive as possible.
* ★ Create environments in your dining room that suit a single guest. A bar where dinner can be ordered works well in some venues, while others have bar-style seating in front of an open kitchen. Depending on your clientele, creating a place where singles can be grouped together might be desirable.
* ★ A bartender with a great gift of gab can be an asset for making singles feel at home if they are in the mood to socialize.
* ★ Managers and owners who greet tables on a regular basis should make an effort to "work" the single diners. Take the time to say hello, but do have a "phone call" to accept if you get cornered by a single diner who wants to have a lengthy discussion.

I've mentioned before that it is much easier to retain a customer than to bring in a new one. Making every type of guest feel at home is really the best investment that you can make in customer satisfaction and future success.

HOLIDAY SERVICE

KEEP YOUR LIFE ON AN EVEN KEEL IN NOVEMBER AND DECEMBER.

For most restaurateurs, the holidays mean a nice, dependable surge in business, but most of the people I know have a tough time getting psyched up every year, because whether they enjoy it or not, the holiday season is stressful for everyone.

Tension Reducers

What can you do to reduce tension at your establishment? Here are a few ideas:

- ★ Review with the staff your policies regarding overindulgent customers. The National Restaurant Association and others offer some wonderful staff-training programs at little or no charge. If you take the time to use them before the holidays begin, everyone gets off to a better start.
- ★ If you have a bar, make sure that your bartenders are trained to watch for potentially problematic situations. Even regular customers can act and respond differently under the emotional pressure of the season.
- ★ Adequate staffing is crucial, so plan accordingly. Avoid, at all costs, coming up short on personnel.
- ★ The reservation book can be either your savior or the source of your undoing. Review reservation policies with everyone in early November so that reservations are kept as accurately as possible. During the holidays, the impact of a lost reservation or a double booking, especially with a large group, is at a maximum. Your stress level will diminish dramatically if you can bank on an accurate reservation book.

Managing Stressful Situations

Here are two holiday dining scenarios. How would you handle them? Have no fear, suggestions follow!

1. Mary and Joe Smith come in with their two kids, accompanied by Joe's in-laws. They have been shopping and fighting crowds for the entire day. The tension level is high, with Joe especially wound up, and the kids are tired and cranky.

   What can a server do to ease this situation? I would recommend engaging Joe as soon as possible. Also, making conversation with the in-laws from out of town can go a long way toward alleviating pressure on both Joe and Mary, allowing Joe to relax and Mary to focus on the kids.

   In addition to the tableside psychology, address their physical needs. Are they thirsty? Is bread on the table ASAP? Is any need that could be quickly handled making itself known? Don't overlook the kids. Make sure that they have something to eat, something to drink, and, if possible, something to do as soon as you can. With practice, you can learn how to add coolant—not fuel—to an overheated table like this.

2. A prestigious law firm is having its holiday party at your restaurant for the first time. You know that these are people who will be very demanding, but the long-term business potential is excellent if they are happy with your service.

   How do you ensure that the party goes perfectly? First of all, the advance knowledge that they are demanding customers is a good thing! You can staff it with your best people, work with your catering manager to make sure that the menu and beverages will work perfectly together, and confirm that you are following all of their requests to the letter. On top of this, make sure that one or two small touches are added that will bring the meal and service up to another level; perhaps an extra appetizer, an added flourish on the dessert, or an extra element of service at some point in the evening would do the trick. As a final closing, a personal thank-you letter from the owner or manager should go to the president of the firm, with a follow-up phone call.

With some planning and foresight, you can make the holidays a little less stressful—and less stress is a gift we can all use!

★ IS IT TIME FOR THE HOLIDAY SEASON ALREADY?

Ready or not, the throngs of harried customers are coming your way, poised to release their stress-induced wrath upon the first person who gets in their way. And, of course, they are all planning large group events at your establishment, including all of the related special needs and wants. The question begs to be asked: Are you ready for them?

Large-Party Stress

What does the holiday season add to traditional large-party service? In a word: pressure. The general stress level is higher than usual as we all try to live up to our own expectations for the holidays and those of family, boss, clients, and friends. To the heightened stress add more merrymaking than usual, and the combination can sometimes lead to unfortunate situations.

Fall is a great time to spend part of a staff meeting reviewing service issues related to overindulging. The folks at TIPS (800-GET-TIPS) have information readily available. Schedule that training today!

How can you work to minimize the holiday pressure on the floor? Realize that everyone else is under the same amount of pressure that you are, and work to avoid taking insults and abuse personally. Remind your staff of the heightened volatility of everyone, and make sure that they also will let customers "vent" without allowing themselves to become victims.

As a manager, asking the right questions in the planning stages of the event can make the execution a piece of cake down the road.

Planning for Success

OK, enough psychology! Let's talk about the mechanics of large-group and banquet service. How does banquet service differ from that of the "regular" table? First, the sheer numbers of guests make the steps of individual table service more difficult. Servers are often working in tandem to accomplish what may normally require only one person to handle. Picture a perfectly tuned, high-performance automobile. Your staff, too, can work efficiently at top speed when planning and staging have been properly done.

As a manager, asking the right questions in the planning stages of the event can make the execution a piece of cake down the road. Working back from the number of guests, talk with the customer about every possible aspect of staging. Aside from the more obvious head table, find out where distinguished guests should be seated. Also, will people be speaking from the tables or moving to a podium? All of the table spacing should allow for easy guest flow.

After the arrangement of the room, think about the staging of the menu. How many courses will there be? Will tables be pre-set for the entire meal or marked between courses? Will any menu items require special plates or silverware?

Large-Group Service

Setting tables for banquets requires all of the precision and flair of a "normal" cover, with the added elements created by the menu, room or staff limitations, and sheer guest numbers. Here are a few general guidelines:

★ Allow 24 to 30 inches between seats. Do not crowd your guests unnecessarily; comfort is a priority!

★ Table basics: one bread service per six guests; one butter service per four guests; one salt/pepper and sugars per six guests; if necessary, one ashtray per four guests.

★ If possible, pre-set all your glassware. It is easier to remove unnecessary glassware than to search for glasses while the event is in progress.

★ If the client is providing centerpieces, make sure that they allow cross-table conversation. If they are interfering, have them gracefully removed.

When I say "banquet service," I know that for many it conjures up a very negative impression of "service for the masses." Remember that the rules of service do not change for large groups. Just think of the large group as individual tables of guests who just happen to be enjoying the same menu on the same schedule!

★ HAPPY HOLIDAY SERVICE!

The holiday season can attract more customers and private parties—and bigger tabs—than any other time of the year. With sharp management and exceptional service, you can have a successful season and build on this business for years to come.

Great Expectations

As always, the secret to good service is understanding the needs of your customers. During the holidays, even more so than during the rest of the year, guests want to celebrate life's delights, including food and wine. And they want to share these pleasures with their families, friends, and business colleagues, so prepare for larger groups. Because the holidays can be stressful, your customers will require additional pampering.

Your job is to live up to their expectations. Let's take a look at three different opportunities to create truly memorable dining experiences for your holiday customers.

1. **Wine List Treasures.** Even in tough economic times, people will splurge at the holidays, especially for higher-priced items perceived as "good values." Look through your cellar and put together a special selection of wines. Older vintages by the glass, a horizontal tasting of great dessert wines, tête de cuvée Champagnes, or even "around the wine world" flights will give your customers a chance to taste fun and interesting selections and share them with friends and family.

   Present wines with a flourish, and serve them in nice stemware. Pouring by-the-glass wines at the table can be terrific theater, especially if you're working with ultrapremium selections. Remember, we are trying to live up to the expectations of the holidays—so put on a performance!

   Don't forget to train your service staff as your restaurant's ambassadors. A staff tasting of the special holiday wines will help build esprit de corps and provide better customer service—a surefire prescription for happier customers and more sales.

2. **Festive Food and Wine Pairings.** Why stop at wine? This is the perfect time of year for your kitchen to create special dishes that showcase skills and ingredients to complement your unique wine selection. Build on the traditional seasonal specialties, but try to make each one a signature dish. Don't forget, your goal is to create an experience your customers will remember (and talk about!) long after the holidays are over.

   Of course, the presentation of your chef's chefs d'oeuvre is as important as the food. Plate spectacular appetizers and flamboyant desserts, and present them with panache.

3. **A Dinner to Remember.** The holidays are also the perfect time to regale your regular customers with a special prix fixe wine-and-food dinner or holiday "package" for their company party. Choose special-event dates well in advance, and select the very best that your kitchen and cellar can deliver. Put on a show, perhaps inviting a winemaker or a charismatic chef as a guest speaker.

   Begin promoting these dinners early, when your customers still have room on their calendars. Your staff should be fully aware of these promotions and eager and prepared to sell them to patrons.

Three Good Reasons

Why go out of your way to bring in more customers if you are already busy during the holidays? Here are three very simple reasons: one, you want to be the best restaurant in town, leading, not trailing, your competition; two, you want to attract and impress both new and core customers—if you perform at your peak, your restaurant's image will be enhanced; and three, you want to give your customers what they want—a special place, with special food and service to match.

Think of this bold approach as an early New Year's resolution. Turn over a new leaf! Attract a new group of desirable customers! Enhance the image of your restaurant for the future! And if you make your guests happy, you will reap the benefits for years to come.

Happy holidays!

American Express Company

Dear Reader,

American Express continues to value the longstanding partnership we've developed with the restaurant industry for more than 35 years. We recognize that the restaurant industry is the cornerstone of our economy and as a key industry partner we continually look for opportunities to help you remain competitive in today's challenging environment.

Delivering valuable educational tools and resources to help restaurateurs is one of our key initiatives. As part of this commitment, American Express has partnered with *Santé, the Magazine for Restaurant Professionals*, and the Allied Domecq Academy of Wine and Service Excellence to bring you, *Five-Star Service: Your Guide to Hospitality Excellence*. This guide is a compilation of best practices and ideas from Evan Goldstein, MS, one of the nation's leading wine and service experts, on how to consistently deliver great hospitality. *Five Star Service* can help you build strategies to make your guests feel special every time and keep them coming back.

American Express knows first-hand the high standards of professionalism and service which are the hallmarks of the restaurant industry. Now more than ever, great service and hospitality are essential to any business's success. Investing resources, both time and money, to properly train all of your employees to provide a superior level of service has great benefits, so we hope this booklet serves as a valuable tool for your business.

We wish you continued success in your establishment and look forward to continuing our partnership with you.

Sincerely,

Scott R. Feldman
Vice President
Restaurant & Entertainment Group
American Express Company

About Allied Domecq Wines USA

Allied Domecq Wines USA is the U.S. fine wine division of Allied Domecq PLC. The California portfolio consists of Atlas Peak Vineyards, Buena Vista Winery, Callaway Coastal, Clos du Bois, Haywood Estate, Mumm Cuvée Napa and William Hill Winery. Allied Domecq Wines USA also manages the US marketing, sales and distribution for Allied Domecq's global wine brands, including Perrier Jouët and Mumm Champagne of France, Cockburn's Port from Portugal, Harveys Bristol Cream and Domecq Sherry from Spain, Bodegas Balbi and Graffigna from Argentina, Brancott Vineyards from New Zealand, and Marques de Arienzo and Bodegas y Bebidas wines from Spain.

About the Allied Domecq Academy of Wine & Service Excellence

The Allied Domecq Academy of Wine & Service Excellence offers practical full-service training and education in wine and dining-room service and business management to help you improve product knowledge and the quality of service you offer your customers.

The Academy is designed to help industry businesses that recognize the necessity of product knowledge and skills but don't necessarily have enough time or resources to fully nurture them. We provide practical and proven business solutions through customized wine and service education for all tiers of the wine and hospitality industry.

Our educational programs are tailored to complement the individual needs of industry professionals ranging from distributors, restaurant and hotel staff, and wine experts to boutique retailers and large corporations. They include single seminars and half- and full-day programs, customized course materials, and practical, proven information and skills your staff can immediately apply to your business. Courses can be held at California-based facilities or we can bring them to you.

The Academy covers all areas of wine, wine business and service, including: wine and winemaking, geographical intensives, restaurant sales and service, food and wine focus, tasting techniques, and business management (tricks of the trade, brand related presentations.)

For more information, please contact us at:
The Allied Domecq Academy of Wine & Service Excellence
375 Healdsburg Avenue, 2nd Floor
Healdsburg, California 95448-4137
Fax: 707-433-3538 or email: adw_academy@adsw.com
Visit our Web site at adw-academy.com.

★ NOTES